# Real-Time Profit Management: Making Your Bottom Line a Sure Thing

**Also from Ernst & Young**

Books for Entrepreneurs:
  *The Ernst & Young Guide to Taking Your Company Public*
  *The Ernst & Young Guide to Financing for Growth*
  *The Ernst & Young Business Plan Guide, Second Edition*

Information Management Series:
  *Development Effectiveness: Strategies for IS Organizational Transition*
  *Managing Information Strategically: Increase Your Company's Competitiveness and Efficiency by Using Information as a Strategic Tool*
  *60 Minute Software: Strategies for Excelerating the IS Delivery System* (forthcoming)
  *Information Technology for Integrated Health Systems: Positioning for the Future* (forthcoming)

General Reference:
  *Privatization: Investing in State-Owned Enterprises Around the World*
  *Mergers & Acquisitions, Second Edition*
  *The Ernst & Young Guide to Total Cost Management*
  *The Ernst & Young Guide to Special Event Management*
  *The Name of the Game: The Business of Sports*
  *The Ernst & Young Almanac and Guide to U.S. Business Cities*
  *Holistic Management* (forthcoming)
  *Real-Time Profit Management: Making Your Bottom Line a Sure Thing*
  *Understanding and Using Financial Data: An Ernst & Young Guide for Attorneys*

Tax & Personal Finance:
  *The Ernst & Young Tax Tax Savers' Guide*
  *The Ernst & Young Tax-Saving Strategies Guide*
  *The Ernst & Young Personal Financial Planning Guide*
  *The Ernst & Young Guide to the New Tax Law*
  *The Ernst & Young New York, New Jersey, Connecticut State Tax Guide*

# Real-Time Profit Management: Making Your Bottom Line a Sure Thing

**Bob Dragoo**

**Ernst & Young LLP**

John Wiley & Sons, Inc.

New York • Chichester • Brisbane • Toronto • Singapore

Library of Congress Cataloging in Publication Data

Real-time profit management:  making your bottom line a sure thing
 / Ernst & Young.
        p. cm.
   Includes bibliographical references
   ISBN 0-471-12617-9 (cloth : alk. paper)
   1. Cost control. 2. Corporate profits. 3. Industrial management.
   4. Reengineering (Management)  I. Ernst & Young.
   HD47.3.r44  1996
   658.15'52—dc20                                        95-14612


Printed in the United States of America

10 9 8 7 6 5 4 3 2 1

To my wife, for her unwavering support and encouragement to write this book.

# Contents

# Preface

The reengineering project has been completed and the CEO is looking for results. You have been summoned to explain why the results can't be in bottom line dollars. You had declared that this project was going to save millions and the CEO had believed you. Where are those savings? Why didn't they appear at the bottom line and stay there as they were supposed to? Today's businesses are seeing the logic in removing the waste and are delving into reengineering projects with fervor, but too many are ignoring the fact that they are in business to make a profit. Even fewer have some form of measurement system in place to tell them how well they are doing at the profit game.

There are ways to capture performance in terms of dollars and cents, even when taking corrective actions against unprofitable events. Two things are absolutely essential in creating this type of management style and responsiveness: receiving the right kind of information and getting that information early enough to do something about it. Today's industry is moving into the twenty-first century with no more than annualized cost data for making tactical decisions.

The results of accumulated and allocated cost information are sufficient for an annualized overview, but they don't do much for making decisions about tight margins on multiple product lines or about whether a particular customer's orders represent profitable business.

We are not oriented toward the *value system* that drives our businesses. We know intuitively what is good and where the big money is made, but do we know where it is *lost?* I believe that there is a distinct discontinuity between the value systems of out shareholders and our middle management. For example, shareholders focus on the return on their investment (either growth or income), while the incentive for most middle managers is volume. Can you imagine why? The reason is that it has been virtually impossible to measure profit. Plant managers have been measured on thruput and then held accountable for their variances from forecast profits. Just ask any plant manager how many days every month he or she uses to figure out why this month's performance in terms of dollars was not on plan.

The discontinuity is clear. Today's financially based measurement systems simply do not offer the right data to the right people in the right time. Consider that financial systems cannot supply any data until the financial period has closed or until all the necessary posting, consolidation and recon-ciliation had been done (at least that is how accountants have explained slow performance in the past). In addition, the data that finally get to the plant manager has been adjusted for credits, taxes, losses, and a host of other accounting adjustments, to the point that it is impossible to tell what the real manufacturing efficiency in converting raw materials to profit was or to determine how to increase profits. The whole point is that not only are the data ineffective as decision sup-port material, but they come far too late to be correlated to the cause of the unexpected behavior. What if a mistake in a blending formula was made, or a weigh scale's calibration was wrong (or any number of common everyday operating mistakes in manufacturing plants were made)? Do those costly errors get flagged in the quarterly financial statement? They do not! Neither the shareholders nor the executives ever even hear about them. Management seldom even discovers them. The plant manager does get to explain to someone that "costs" were a little higher than expected.

Suppose that you could continuously measure the profitability of each and every product you make at the very time it is being made. Transpose that into sales/order slate and you could then tell the profitability of every order you produced. Every customer's profitability contribution could be known. Do you think that with this information you might be able to make better decisions about the production schedule, about the pricing strategy, about the product slate, and about the focus of cost reduction programs within the organization? Need I ask more? Having pertinent data, in real time, is going to be the biggest change in management of the bottom line ever to sweep industry. You can't manage profit if you can't measure it, and those measurements must be available in time to take corrective action to avoid a loss.

Now, about that reengineering project that was supposed to generate a change to the bottom line. Do you suppose that no measures were put in place to determine a baseline to provide direction to the team that employed those reengineering methodologies? Do you suppose that the team reengineered process that had little impact on the bottom line? Was its focus on volume or on cost? We have data from a large number of reengineering projects that tell us many reengineering projects were disappointing to their corporate sponsors, with bottom line results not as much as was expected. Could it be that once the focus of attention shifts, behavior slip right back to the old paradigm? Measurements can be used like a ratchet, to prevent backsliding of improvements. There are many reasons to install measurements that are pertinent when focused on the value element that is crucial to bottom line performance: *profit!*

This book is about what can be done after reengineering to capture the same effect as locking in the ratchet on a socket wrench or on a fishing reel. Never let a good behavior or improvement slip backwards, and always give people information that is meaningful to the performance of the business. Make those process improvements connect to bottom line performance by measuring them in terms of profit contribution and behavior. Know whether you are doing "well" right now, so you can take credit in the profitable times and avoid the unprofitable.

In the financial world, we have long understood the relationship between time and cash flow. We have even made a science of the "time-value of money," learning how to establish the value (or penalty) of uncollected cash or investments. The independent variable that drives this decision-making process is time.

As we install and begin to use the new hardware and software systems, learn some of the new methods of business process reengineering, and adapt our organizations toward improved quality and higher performance, we *must not* overlook the contribution that time can have. It plays a key role in the design of pertinent performance measures and decision support tools.

Consider the element of time in the field of medicine. In certain traumas, time can mean the difference between life and death. In most diagnosis and treatment methodologies, time is a major consideration in the determination of cause and effect. But in today's industry, the all-important measurement, the bottom line, comes to us only after all the spending has been accounted for and after many have had a chance to work their magic or make a few adjustments to structure and content. In too many cases the answer to the question, "How did we do?" comes weeks after the events that actually created those results. One way to practice a true form of managing the bottom line is to collapse the time cycle of pertinent tactical and strategic profitability measurements.

The creation and definition of tools and measures for making profits manageable is the purpose of this book.

Technology has reached a point of supporting the acquisition, consolidation, calculation, and presentation of costs, sales, and profit information by product, by customer, by order, by region, and so on. The marriage of sensor-based measurements of certain consumables with activity-based costing models now enables feedback of this type of information in virtual real time. This form of decision support can be used in both short-term tactical and in strategic ways. The major benefit seems to come in the strategic arena for planning product mix, minimum order size, profitability by customer and by order—all in time to make decisions without the risk of "sunk" costs.

Time is an incredibly valuable component of the management decision-making process. The availability of strategic (and tactical) measurements in time to avoid costly excursions into business scenarios previously presumed "safe," but later labeled as "variances," has finally arrived.

This book introduces a new concept in business process management: the use of cost and profit measurements as control variables and as strategic business-planning parameters. Using costs to support executive and operating decisions has been going on for years, but the source (financial systems) of that data provides only averaged and delayed results. Technology now permits rapid access to the many sources of information needed for the measurement and calculation of costs. The fundamental difference between current cost accounting systems and this new concept is *time*. Conventional systems collect, summarize, and allocate spending after some period of time. This new concept measures and displays costs (and in an associated form, profit) as they are consumed—in real time.

When the highway patrol officer stops you for speeding, you know that your speed was *measured* with radar—in real time. You would *never* argue that you had only driven an *average* of

55 mph over the last quarter, but that is exactly the analogy to how we manage our businesses when we use the information from conventional cost accounting systems. This book defines a way to integrate some of your existing (and perhaps require a few new) business and manufacturing sources to provide a new dimension in managing profit.

# CHAPTER 1

# How We Got to This Point

In 1968, I was challenged to design and build a process control system that would optimize a major processing unit in a large refinery. Planning Systems were in their infancy, but I knew that I would have to learn how to utilize that tool to find the optimum targets for control. I finally succeeded in developing a model of the process, mated it to the best planning tool I could find, and was ready to demonstrate my prowess at optimizing process control when my client, who was 30 years my senior, asked me, in a fatherly way, how I knew that maximum thruput was equal to maximum profit. Well, I didn't, but I didn't want to let him know that; so I took a flow diagram of the unit and a material balance showing design flow rates. I began the task of creating what would become a cost model—not dissimilar from what we, today, call an *activity-based model*. It took me quite a while to capture and convert all the measurements I needed into common units of measure

1

compatible with the unit costs I cajoled and discovered from a variety of sources. The final result was an ability to calculate the actual manufacturing cost of the product being created in this unit. Then I took the contract selling price of that product and calculated the profit. Of course, this was a gross profit number, not yet burdened with overheads and support expenses, but it was an indicator of performance that held some enormous surprises for me, revealing that the profit versus volume curve was not a straight line.

I cycled the profit calculation every 30 seconds and filtered the output through a "running average" calculation to even out the resultant. Then I sent that value through an analog (voltage) output terminal to a 12" square meter that I had an artist friend modify so that the scale read in units of profit (Exhibit 1.1).

Of course, I did all this to prove the point that my thruput optimization also created maximum profit. Imagine my disappointment when I discovered that peak profitability came at a point *far* sooner than peak production. This experience became part of my learning curve in measuring efficiency. The drama had not yet reached its climax, however.

With some integration of cost modeling as input to a second-generation planning model, and with appropriate data captured directly from the process control system, the

**(Exhibit 1.1)**   Profit Meter

goal I had hoped for—acceptance by my client, now turned mentor—seemed closer than ever.

Then came the greatest surprise and twist yet. I decided to observe unit operations in the control center after hours, actually to go out to the plant and spend a few hours watching my creation calculate the profits produced during this production cycle. Well, the surprise came when the third shift came on and promptly ignored (actually turned the controls *off*) the directions generated by my creation—they wanted to run the unit by watching the profit meter. After all, management was interested in bigger profits, and this way the workers could learn how to fine-tune the unit by watching the profit meter every time they tried something. I never would have believed that they could out perform my optimizer, but they did. They knew things about how that unit reacted that have never been written in a book. They knew how a rain shower cooled it, how fresh catalyst ran, and how to "hear" a pump beginning to fail. All that the conventional measures feeding the process control system could do was to track those subtle changes. My optimization model could never predict them, but those operators could. Their intuition and experience combined with a brand new form of pertinent performance feedback gave them the ability to achieve profitability totals beyond anything our closed-loop system had done.

I began to understand that operating with the ultimate performance measurement—profit contribution—was the only way I could show tangible benefits from my attempts at process control. After all, dollars do drive the economy. So, why not enhance this unique concept of managing production, with one important new process variable—profit?

It took many years and some introductions into how to run a business to truly begin to appreciate the value, both strategic and tactical, of not only having measurements of profitability, but also (1) having them available in time to avoid long trips into the red ink; (2) having performance histories and analyses of profitability by product, by location, by customer; and (3) making strategic decisions about how to steer a business toward improved profits, and then keeping it there.

I had discovered a valuable new tool and I had discovered it the way many great discoveries are made—by accident—while I was trying to prove something else.

What was the key element of this new concept of "measured profitability"? It was (and is) a faster time frame for the availability of the measurement. In the preface, you read my analogy of the speeder who argued that she drove an average of 55 mph. The elements that make that example correlate with real-life cost accounting systems are the dimensions that create the "average" factor: *time,* lots of it, and results long after the fact.

Conventional cost accounting systems accumulate spending over some extended period of time and then use a variety of allocation techniques to spread that long-term accumulation of spending across certain elements of the business—surprisingly enough, not always by product or by customer.

Let's look back at the beginning of cost accounting and see what we can learn from its genesis.

Publicly owned corporations are required to keep financial records according to certain minimum standards. These requirements are well established and enforced by law, but they don't include any cost accounting. Cost accounting evolved as those who were asked to strategically manage the business understood that certain types of cost data were absolutely necessary for them to be able to steer a business toward profitability. Those businesses that manufactured a variety of products in the same plants (such as small appliances, toys, packaged foods, beverages, auto parts, electronic goods, and hundreds of other variety product slated companies) especially suffered from the inherent flaws in a financially-based cost accounting system.

We need to understand how conventional cost accounting

systems work in order to discover their shortcomings for use in day-to-day strategic business decisions. Financial systems accumulate spending over a period of time. This sum becomes the quantity that will be allocated back into the various cost centers defined by the cost accountant. Now, there's nothing fundamentally wrong with using accumulated spending and total volumes of production to come up with unit costing, as long as *averaged* results are acceptable; a sum divided by a quantity of goods can produce only an average result. Now consider the period of time this average spans. One month is the shortest period and three months is more typical. This means you will see no trends or movement in cost that occur, then disappear, during this measurement period.

Let's look at both sides of the costing equation: spending and production quantity. Have you ever known a business that didn't have write-offs, credits, carry-overs, and other revenue adjustments? What do you suppose such adjustments do to the purity of the spending side of the equation? So, to begin with, the accuracy of the actual spending is in doubt.

Production costs are not as subject to question if you make only one product. But what if your time period is used to make 3, 10, or 30 different products? Ever wonder how to divide up the spending then? Most often, businesses have developed a set of standards that represent the theoretical or design-basis amount of production time required to produce each product. Then they count the total production and normalize the standards to total production time. Each product's standard has now been "factored" one way or the other and the spending is divided by total units to give average unit cost. That is multiplied by the adjusted standard (factor) to represent the product's fair share of cost.

What might a technique like that miss? Can you imagine any differences in productivity between assembly workers? Or suppose a piece of equipment is getting a little dull and isn't producing as fast as usual. Perhaps the supplier for your raw materials just upped the price on the product and your clerk is a few weeks behind getting all that data into your cost system. Maybe you had some quality problems and some percentage of your production had to be reworked to meet spec.

A cost accountant might ponder:

"Should I use the utility bill I got this month (for the period of 6 weeks ago) for this month's financials or should I use the dollars I actually paid out, or should I try to measure my usage and guess how much the utility is going to charge me? I'm always confused—maybe if I'll just be consistent it won't matter."

Such real-life events happen every day and decrease confidence in the use of standards for calculating unit cost.

What about the timing of available results? I have never heard of a financial system closing on the last day of the month (or quarter). It always takes days or weeks before all those adjustments mentioned earlier have been argued over and resolved. Therefore, costing data could be available weeks after some nonstandard event that happened on the very first day of that financial period. Weeks-old information has very little value for a manager or business owner. It is almost impossible to correlate cause and effect when variations occur from period to period.

How many dozens of other timing flaws exist in the most basic elements of our costing systems? Certainly, no one ever deliberately designed a cost accounting system without taking lots of care and thought to overcome the inherent flaws described here. And many come really close to being accurate in some regards. Few, unfortunately, ever come close to giving cost information when it was needed to reposition the business's course and keep it on track. Unfortunately, manufacturing executives have to keep an eye on other performance indicators such as yield, production, backlog, and inventory to trigger a concern that something is amiss.

How did we get to a point of improved cost calculation? In the early 1980s, a great deal of attention was focused on the manufacturing industries. That focus was to try and combine the power and speed of computers with the manufacturing and business support processes to achieve higher levels of performance through integration.

The terms "computer integrated manufacturing" and "computer aided manufacturing" came into vogue. Integrated manufacturing information systems touched many aspects of the manufacturing business and were taken up as *causes* by such organizations as Computer Aided Manufacturing International (CAM-I). The application of information technology benefited production planning, material movements, and customer service. The concept of linking corporate goals (improved profits) to the manufacturing floor, through integrated systems, was born during this period.

CAM-I, under the leadership and inspiration of one man, Jim Brimson, developed a way to link the troublesome problem of *managing the bottom line* to the shortcomings in existing cost accounting methodologies. That linkage was the key that allowed Jim Brimson to lead a task force of industry experts to develop an implementable methodology: activity-based costing. This concept of looking at the individual steps of the manufacturing process as a series of activities made it possible to measure cost as it was consumed and to accurately compile the costs of each product made.

This concept was to be the key to creating a bridge from corporate goals to hourly and daily decision making. Before that, the "us" versus "them" distinction was obvious to me when I worked in a plant's manufacturing group. We often spoke of the financial group up in the "ivory tower" who had no clue as to what was "really going on." Yet they had the audacity to visit monthly and demand that our manufacturing group explain our variances from their carefully calculated, unrealistic forecasts and standards. (I later became part of that "ivory tower" after I was promoted into the management ranks and had to switch over to the other side of the table. It was a difficult transition, as you might well imagine.)

Now, however, these pioneering concepts from CAM-I are beginning to revolutionize the way we make decisions about the strategic direction of a business. In this context, *strategic actions* are those that are mandatory to achieve success. Today's computer technology permits a number of data sources to join together toward a common solution, enabling these concepts to become reality.

My thesis is to go beyond activity-based costing (ABC), adding another dimension to this integrated solution: measuring the *cost drivers* in real time. Capture the measurements of those materials, utilities, and activities that impact a large portion of the cost—as they happen—and report an activity-based cost, as frequently as it makes sense, to those who can take corrective actions. The tactical benefit of knowing how well you are doing at any given moment (feedback) enables an operating group to minimize costly waste. The value in this concept of real-time costing will be the subject of a later chapter.

The ability to identify and capture the cost of each major activity and report it as a recorded control variable is revolutionary. It links operations and support services with the business goal of making a profit through a connection not available before. Finally, it provides a "speedometer" measurement of how well the business is doing that can be seen at a glance. Note that a new dimension has been introduced. That new dimension, within the reporting of cost, is *time*.

## CHAPTER 1 HIGHLIGHTS:

A.  An accidental discovery of how cost feedback had value.

B.  Understanding and appreciating the contribution of operators.

C.  Profit as a control variable.

D.  A description of conventional cost accounting systems.

E.  The inception of activity-based costing.

# CHAPTER 2

# The Revolution

As a result of the concepts discussed in Chapter 1, it is possible to say: "Now I can measure profit."

Profit was always a resultant, a piece of news that was delivered by your accountant. I always felt apprehension, excitement, and a surge of fear when my financial representative appeared with "the news." I always tried to read his face, check out his body language. I even listened for the speed of his footsteps for a clue. I was, forever, the optimist, and hoped for good news.

I knew from tracking proposals and contract closings; from watching production and yield efficiency; and from tracking raw material costs, labor production efficiency, and fixed costs, where we should be. But, somehow, several days near the end of each financial period were spent trying to reconcile *why* reality and expectations seldom agreed. Naturally, I passed all blame on to those under me, requiring them to face the inevitable inquisition. (Ever wonder why plant managers buy antacids by the case?) I finally realized that I didn't know how to be proactive about managing profit. The production manager was driven daily to make a target volume, which was measured, but he was held accountable for profit, *which wasn't.*

As the need to measure profit began to be recognized, many attempts to do so were tried. Today, computer and communications technology has reached a point of evolution that permits the combining of the many types and sources of information necessary to achieve this end-point performance measurement that is so important to the lifeblood of a business.

In Chapter 1, we talked about the old way that profitability was derived from spending and production. We also described how ABC has been recognized as an improved way of measuring what really goes on in the manufacturing areas, with regard to the consumption of individual elements of cost. But the real key difference between having the information and getting *value* from it is this: *when* you get the information and *how* you respond to it. So, timing and action are key elements of the value of improved knowledge about your operation.

## Case History

Company X produces 800 million pounds of finished product a year. Its business consists of a batch system feeding a continuous process, which is 94% to 96% loaded and then flows into a packaging area that is 74% to 76% loaded. The product mix is broad, consisting of about 40 different base products, and is split between several high-volume, short manufacturing cycle products and a number of low-volume, long manufacturing cycle specialty products that command a 25% premium in price.

The current cost accounting system accurately considers most costs. However, the breakout of individual product costs is done by a finished goods volume allocation method, which distributes average costs across each pound of finished product. Evaluation of utilized assets reveals that some specialty products take as much as four times as long in the continuous process area as standard products do. They also utilize more expensive raw materials, and their low-volume orders consume a higher percentage of setup and cleanup time.

Management was considering the strategic question of whether or not to pursue more specialty business, because of the 25% price premium that could be realized. Because the current cost accounting system averages most of the costs associated with production, the accounting department's conclusion was to pursue the specialty business, arguing that the pricing premium was money in the bank.

The real answer requires a more accurate understanding of the actual cost comparisons of standard versus specialty products. Each product's *real* cost is a function of its consumption of raw materials, variable resources consumed, and relative effectiveness in using the manufacturing facilities to produce product. An activity-based costing methodology was utilized to provide a more realistic representation of the costs of finished products. This method was implemented in real time to provide a history for support of both tactical and strategic business decisions. Implementation of the real-time cost variables enabled operators to act tactically on cost variances before they became sunk costs—costs that already have been spent before you discovered the mistake. It also enabled them to identify the cost of excess quality and the penalty (in cost) of operating in a "comfort zone" in process control. These pieces of information enabled operators to lower product cost by several percentage points.

In this case, the application of *real-time cost management* tools also revealed, strategically, that even a 25% price premium did not cover the true costs of the specialty products. It further revealed that the current product mix was consuming inordinate amounts of the continuous process time, leaving the packaging area underutilized. A shift in product mix, away from specialty products, created a 50 million pound per year increase in available capacity (6.2%) and improved bottom line profitability by several percentage points.

Operators are now working under an incentive plan, and are enjoying the benefits of being able to contribute directly to improved profitability. Employees can see the direct application of several years of quality programs, by being empowered with information and control over product cost—an issue so important to corporate success.

## Using Real-time Cost Information

You see, value comes in different ways. Improved knowledge and resolution of detail can help you make strategic changes in the way you direct and manage your business. But *when* you get the information is as important as the content of that information. (The fact that I bet on the wrong horse would be worth a lot more to me before I bet the money than after.)

The technology revolution, which evolved over a period of a few years, has genuinely broken down the barriers to gaining value from cost information. We must begin to make some revolutionary changes in our thought processes to discover how to harvest the full value from this timely and important new form of measurement.

We have all just barely learned what a paradigm is, and now we must break ours, because of the new kinds of data that are available. (A paradigm is the normal practice that has been accepted and is in habitual use.) Most of us have probably had trouble learning how to use new things (for example, VCRs), and cost has not been a measured control variable before. What should we expect? How should we react to dynamic cost moves? Can we use these data to motivate workers?

Will we be able to make changes if we discover that some products don't make any profit?

Many more questions will arise as we get into the planning phase of this approach. Personally, I believe that the concept can be taken to the extreme. I actually know one person who measured the cost of group meetings and ran a calculator display of the accumulated dollars burned to try to get groups to pursue value in return for the cost of the meeting. But we all know that "when three or more are gathered to make a decision, the cost will be more than you want to know." So don't attempt to use cost in a heavy-handed way to change everything all at once.

We have learned that the 80/20 rule (20% of the activities will cause 80% of the problems) can be applied in making major direction and strategy decisions. So you need to focus only on the major items to make a big difference in the way your business performs (Exhibit 2.1).

It is revolutionary to be able to see profit by product, but by using technology, you can get that information today—in fact, you can get it in such resolution that you can see the variability in cost between a small order and a large order of the same product. You can actually plot the cost of startup, price the amount of off-specification material made at the beginning of a new production run, and calculate the point at

**(Exhibit 2.1)** Profit by Product

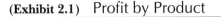

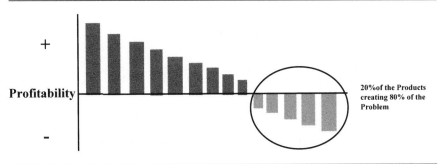

Profitability

20%of the Products creating 80% of the Problem

which you offset the losses from startup (breakeven). It is also revolutionary to know how to set minimum order size based on the actual ability to make a profit on a product. (Ask yourself the question: Do you sell many small lots?)

I have one customer for whom 75% of his clients make up only 1% of his revenue. I was immediately suspicious that his transaction costs and inventory carrying costs were more than the profit from sales to these small orders. (And I hadn't counted cost of goods sold yet.) Countless times, I have seen product mixes that both make a profit and take it away, with a net profit that seems unpredictable and is hard to explain simply because some products are not profitable at all, or are not profitable in the order size being produced.

Not too long ago, Wall Street recognized a significant turnaround by a major electronics manufacturer and quizzed the new president about how the turnaround was accomplished. The reply was that activity-based costing had been the basis of a product profitability analysis, allowing the company to retire those products that were unprofitable. It's wonderful how profits improve when you're not trying to add negative numbers to that important profit column.

Two parts of that business performance recovery are noteworthy: one, that factual information was made available in a timely manner and two, that *action* was taken.

Remember: Value isn't really value until it becomes *fact* and action is always required to create fact.

## CHAPTER 2 HIGHLIGHTS:

    A. Change of profit from a reported result to a control variable.

    B. Cost control as a new concept.

    C. Time is a crucial element in decision making.

D. Focus on time and cost control made possible by technology revolution.

E. Unprofitable products both subtract dollars *and* consume production time that could have been used to make profitable contributions.

F. Information gained from a focus on measured costs.

# CHAPTER 3

# 50 Years of Control

The premise of this book is that a new variable can be created to support the process of profit management. This variable is *measured cost*. The path to a realistic calculation of cost is a complex, but entirely realistic one. The ability to calculate cost in real time has a profound influence on removing barriers for managing the profit-generating capability of manufacturing businesses.

In order to understand how ongoing and frequent measurements of cost can be used to make tactical and strategic decisions about the mix of products, the distribution of products into different markets, and the profitability of individual customer orders, you need to be introduced to the fundamentals of process control.

This chapter focuses on a review of the basic concepts of process control, how they evolved, and how they relate to the application of cost measurements and profit management decision support. It is also important to understand the analogy between overhead costs for a business process and a manufacturing process.

## Manufacturing and Process Control

In a manufacturing process, raw materials are converted into higher valued, more complex products through the steps of mixing, blending, conversion, reaction, machining, or a hundred other possible actions. Each of these manufacturing steps must be carefully managed (controlled) in order to produce repeatable quality and consistent content. Let's examine a rudimentary manufacturing step and see how process control is used (Exhibit 3.1).

Early in the industrial revolution, this type of manufacturing step might have been carried out by measuring weight or volume. Volume will be used here for illustration. Typically a measurement tank would hold the mixture before it was released into the mixing tank, allowing a visual measurement of how much volume is drawn (remember the old gas pumps in which a few gallons would be pumped up into the measurement tank, then released into your car?). Exhibit 3.2 shows this process.

This technique required a person—commonly referred to as an *operator*—to pay careful attention to the manual valve

**Exhibit 3.1**    Basic Mixing Process

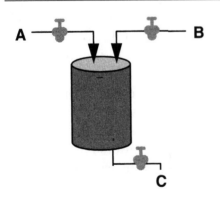

Product C is made
by mixing 2 parts of
"A" with 1 part of "B".

**Exhibit 3.2** Mixing Process with Measurement Tank

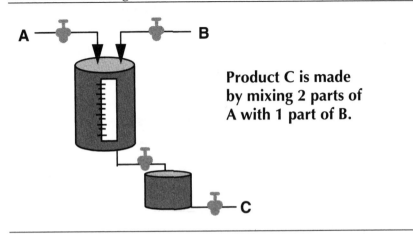

**Product C is made
by mixing 2 parts of
A with 1 part of B.**

control. The accuracy of each blend would be entirely dependent on the commitment to attention and accuracy by the
operator. In reality, repeatability (process accuracy) was not
high and improved methods of measurement and control
were sought.

Every form of manufacturing depended on the quality of
work performed by the craftsperson. Higher volume and
fewer workers caused the quality of the work product to suffer.
Incidences of operator error in manual operations historically
ran as high as 5 to 10%. Today the incidence of error in manual operations remains high.

It becomes clear that sensors to perform the measurement
and automated devices to control the rate of consumption
were to become the focus of the industrial control system's
world. Indeed, large corporations such as Foxboro, Honey-
well, and Taylor grew out of this need, and in the 1930s and
1940s, they began to supply the manufacturing industry with
automated systems that both measured and controlled—
allowing the selection of target amounts to be preset and,
even better, allowing the simultaneous flow of multiple products,

**Exhibit 3.3**   Automated Mixing Process

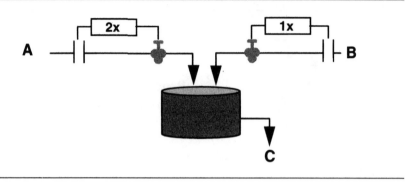

at a measured rate, into the mixing tank (Exhibit 3.3).

This point in the evolution of process control allowed a continuous flow of product to be continuously adjusted for the proper ratio of components. At first these control devices were pneumatic (powered by air), then in the 1950s and 1960s they evolved into electronic technology, basically constructed to emulate the old pneumatic control. By the late 1960s and early 1970s, digital concepts began to be applied and process variables were being managed singly and in multiples by digital control algorithms. This new technology was known as *supervisory control systems*. Today, digital technology permits hands-off control of many manufacturing steps because the measurement and control actions within a manufacturing process can be accomplished with available technology.

But, and this is the key to this book, even today, we continue to use this highly evolved technology of process control to perform the same functions it did 50 years ago: measure and manage flows of raw materials, manufacturing conditions (pressure, temperature, etc.), and quality through the feedback of test instruments that can measure important characteristics of the finished product.

Now our shareholders are interested in how much profit we generate—consequently, our executives live (and die) by the code of profits. They have to stand before the board of directors and explain how their executive leadership contributed (or much worse, did not contribute) to profits from the business they were responsible for managing. But, there is a break in the line of accountability between the executive suite and the operating groups. I almost always find that manufacturing is held accountable for volume—not for profitability of the product. In addition, operators have probably never even heard of a need to understand profit in their minute-to-minute, hour-to-hour regimen of managing their part of the manufacturing process (Exhibit 3.4).

This *disconnect* in the business process is one of the most important of today's business issues: profits are not managed; they are merely the result of a planned operation. Good exec-

**Exhibit 3.4**  Difference in Leadership Motivation

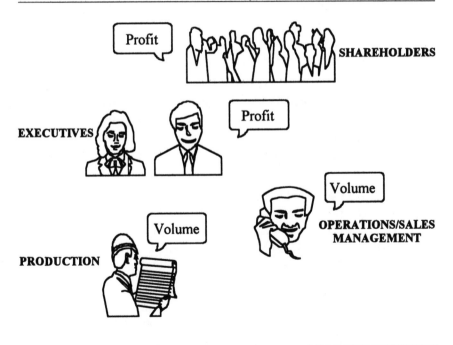

utives have understood this for a long time and have worked hard to derive good plans, improve on them, and adapt to indicators using feedback available from financial reporting. Operations departments have worked hard to track the plan more closely, to be more predictable, and to reduce the number of off-specification products. The norm has been to plan to be profitable and hope that goal is achieved.

Today, measurements exist for a bridge to bring profit measurement into the process control world as a new control variable. Imagine an operator having a target for profitability and being able to glance at his or her profit meter and see if the goal is being met.

W. Edwards Deming[1] taught us to take appropriate accountabilities and push them down to the level of the person who runs the machines. That theory works only if the person in control of the action that consumes cost has some feedback measurement to show where he or she is in relation to the target.

Why has cost (the root element to profit is cost) been overlooked? Our paradigm of a manufacturing organization has been to put the cost accounting function up in the front office, with the accounting group. Perhaps if that group had been located out in the control room or in the manufacturing area, this disconnect would never have happened. Today manufacturing costs are not *in control*—they are simply accounted for, after the fact.

I am suggesting that we already measure the consumption of raw materials. We measure energy, production rates, and most of the elements of the cost of the product. They already exist. Of course, fixed costs are well known and can be

---

[1]Dr. W. Edwards Deming (Oct. 14, 1900–Dec. 20, 1993) is the industrial management expert who was credited with teaching post-WWII Japanese industrialists quality control techniques that enabled Japan to triumph over U.S. auto makers in the 1980s.

assigned through some of these measurements (for example, production rate can tell how much of a fixed asset is used in the production of a product).

What is missing are the unit costs of these consumed materials and activities (here, at last, is the genesis of the term "activity-based costing"). In the past few years, information technology (hardware, communications, and software) has evolved to the point of being able to link and share pertinent information. The combination of a process control measurement with financial data was a hard obstacle to overcome for most cultures, but as the value of that combination is better understood, the application of a real-time profit calculation will grow to be the single most important business process control variable.

Process control has evolved through 50 years of technological advance. Reliability, accuracy, and automation of the highest order have evolved to manage the classic elements of process control more effectively. I am suggesting that we pursue a revolutionary step in control: the marriage of measured cost drivers with the raw cost data and selling prices, in order to provide our hands-on operators with the tactical feedback they need to keep their activity as profitable as possible.

Process control is a highly tactical activity. All of the value from real-time cost knowledge is not tactical, however. An enormous amount of knowledge can be gleaned from study of the cost (and profit) behavior—that is, what makes it change? Many discoveries are made about margins on specific products that were thought to have been one thing, but discovered to be another. Discoveries about the profitability of certain markets, plants, and lines often tend to alter the strategy of business—Chapters 9 and 10 address this issue.

# CHAPTER 3 HIGHLIGHTS:

A. Measured cost as a process control variable.

B. Review of basic concepts of measurement and feedback.

C. Evolution of ability to measure consumptions.

D. Linkage of consumptions to cost drivers.

# CHAPTER 4

# The Dynamics of Cost Data

When we think of costing results in a classical way, we focus on the answer to the question, "Well, how much did it cost?" We let the excitement of the end result overcome the intrinsic value in what is happening moment by moment in the consumption of the manufacturing and support activities. I've already stated that there are good and bad days in controlling costs.

Let's set a basis from which we can examine the dynamics of cost data. Raw materials make up a significant part of the cost of most manufactured products. The next largest cost item is usually those activities that convert the raw material to its finished form. Remember the 80/20 rule—focus on the 20% of the activities that contain 80% of the variance or value.

The accurate measurement of consumption should be another focus. Simply taking the total at the end of the month may be acceptable for tracking inventory, but you will over-

:h of the value if you don't track, log, and learn from ages in cost and try to discover what causes the change _ sumption as the process moves along. Input and output rates should correlate closely. *Yield* is the classical method of tracking the efficiency changes in many manufacturing processes. Not until we put cost into the yield thought process do we begin to capture the importance of understanding just how the costs move around.

The manufacturing processes are usually the cause for the most variation in yield. When the process is perfect, yield is at its peak. The more complex the process, the more things can be imperfect and the degrees of variance are infinite. Most processes include dozens of major potential problems. Operators will quickly tell you that some variations cannot be explained. Some of the known causes include season of the year, and minute difference in raw materials from different sources. Others are related to the age of the product or the purity of the component. What we need to understand is how these variations impact our cost and that requires an examination of more than the totals presented at the end of the month.

In order to capture the value from analysis of this dynamic, it is imperative to have access to a history of information about key cost drivers. This data must include the time each data point was recorded, so we can complete our analysis. The analysis allows us to correlate cause and effect. Time becomes the synchronizing factor that allows us to see how a fall in purity can cause a fall in yield (Exhibit 4.1).

A study of the changes that occur in the measurements of the drivers of our cost activities will help to prepare us for the amount of variation we should expect from our activity-based cost equations when calculated as frequently as hourly. Thus, if your cost drivers demonstrate visible movement, your cost will have one too. Is that bad? No, but it is a problem for those of us who only wanted to know "the answer." It is almost as if

**Exhibit 4.1**   Trends of Performance

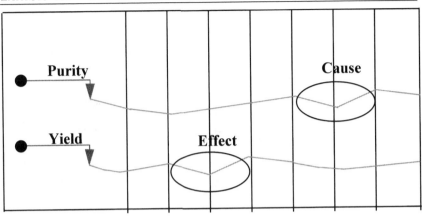

we can't make up our mind because the answer keeps changing. The truth is that things change all the time.

How can we manage the result so that change isn't discon-
certing? Several methods are typically used to moderate the
frequency and speed of movement, without taking away the
benefit of knowing that a cost is trending away from target.
One method is a *rolling average:* taking the current value and
averaging it with the last 10, 20, or 50 values to smooth out the
fluctuations that come from frequent calculation of cost. I
prefer to continue the fast-cycle calculation and filter results
rather than slow down the cycle-time of the calculation itself.
(Cycle-times don't have to be measured in seconds. Minutes
or hours, however, will never overload a computer.) When
results are filtered this way, the output can be plotted in a
smooth curve.

Another technique for tracking trends is to take 5, 10, or
15 calculations and analyze them statistically as a *sample set.*
Look at the average, the variance, and other statistical proper-
ties of the sample. Then plot the statistical values to see how
well the subject is in control.

**Exhibit 4.2** Cost Components

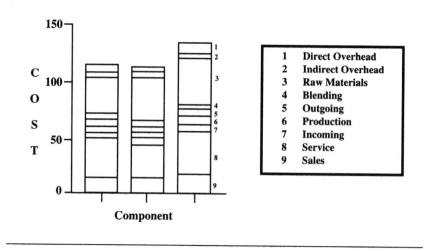

Component

I am an advocate of learning both what drives my cost and of how well each activity is under control. I get a good clue as to where I need to invest in education or improvements in the process when I see a lot of variance in the measured cost of an activity.

Remember, the total cost is the sum of many activities; some have significant dynamics and some have little or no dynamic. Depreciation of fixed assets doesn't change, but the productivity of a shift worker does. The fact that some of the cost elements don't change dramatically doesn't mean that you won't benefit from running the cost model at a frequency that correlates with the fastest moving activity! The sum of the parts is still going to show you how your cost reacts to those activities you *can* do something about (Exhibit 4.2). That's what this method is all about—providing new information in a time frame that allows you to react and correct the process in order to move toward an improved profit position.

The acceptance of cost as a control variable permits a whole new range of management functions: tactical actions for corrective moves and responsive changes to trends that cost money. Strategic actions taken after learning that certain schedules, products, rates, policies, and techniques generate less profit than desired and can be circumvented by better planning utilize the knowledge gained from ABC.

Cost data dynamics are often overlooked as a valued component of the ABC program, but a great deal can be learned from them about what is contributing to the poor average performance of a manufacturing or support process.

## CHAPTER 4 HIGHLIGHTS:

    A. Variances shown by frequent calculation of cost.

    B. Correlation between cause and effect.

    C. Acceptability of variance.

    D. Filtering to smooth results.

    E. Intrinsic tactical and strategic value in dynamics of cost measurement.

# CHAPTER 5

# The Importance of a Time-History

All too often, we focus on the destination or end product and overlook the value of what we can learn along the way. I learned, from a very wise mentor, that a great deal of knowledge can be gained by paying attention to the events along the route toward a destination. His habit was to enjoy the journey, not to pine for the destination. The forms of rapid transportation developed during the twentieth century have produced a generation that has never experienced the pleasure of a leisurely journey. Indeed, in more than a half-century of my own life experiences, I can seldom recall any travel when I wasn't under some time constraint to reach an appointed destination. I can only dream of taking a train for the pure pleasure of it or a tramp steamer for casual travel to a foreign land. The lessons learned along the way do have value. Harvesting that value is our goal; gaining every benefit possible from our organization is our obligation to the stockholders whose investments we are responsible for tending. (How many times do we lose sight of this obligation?)

I have always admired the occasional businessperson I have encountered who can look at a spreadsheet or some page full of numbers and see some hidden fact embedded in the relationships of one set of numbers to another. Those special people seem to be looking into some crystal ball when they gaze into seemingly innocuous numbers and pluck out a conclusion that a supplier must have overcharged or that the catalyst in the reactor must have lost its designed activity level. How do they see those things? Do they have millions of pieces of data floating around in their heads and this particular number makes the picture complete? Perhaps, but the real answer is that they can visualize trends. They have the ability to graph mentally a history of some performance measurement and come up with a recognition of some discontinuity or of some deviation from the expected.

I've tried to learn how to do this over the years, but I have discovered that I need help. I've learned to keep a running record (history) of important measures that relate to my business. For example, productivity per employee, backlog, overhead percentage, and volume of outstanding proposals have long been business performance indicators that help keep things on track.

When I get business performance measures like these, I have several ways to gain value from them. I can simply examine the magnitude and determine whether it is within acceptable limits (Exhibit 5.1). Forecasted performance is the basis of acceptance in many business decisions. But the plotting of a time-history (the "journey" of that measure) can give me a wealth of additional information.

Suppose you saw the trend in Exhibit 5.2. Would you be better informed? I would be provoked to some level of concern, assuming the trend was continuing to move in the negative business direction.

**Exhibit 5.1**   Operating Within Acceptable Limits

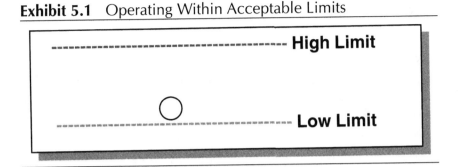

My point is that the creation of a historical database of the major components of your business performance measurements allows you to gain value from the intrinsic information contained within those data's behavior. Your visualization will benefit from the truth in that old adage "a picture is worth a thousand words." A time-history yields direction, rate of change, length of time to reach the limit, probability of recovery, correlation of cause and effect, and many other intuitive conclusions not easily ascertained from the classic single data point report.

If I had the gift of visualization, I might not need the pictorial representation, but I find that a graph or plot of the historical behavior is essential. I truly need to understand the behavior of a piece of my business before I can establish a strategy for correcting a problem.

**Exhibit 5.2**   Direction of Movement Within Limits

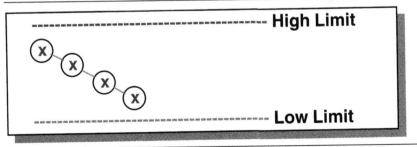

# TIME-HISTORY

Just what is a time-history? Suppose I capture a piece of information but have no idea which period of time it represents. I would have difficulty being able to determine a course of action. Knowledge of the precise time of that sample gives me the ability to correlate the influences that may have impacted that performance. So I ask that a pertinent piece of additional information be captured with all critical performance measurements: time. I call this process time stamping. A familiar example is the stamping of the time on the ticket you receive when entering a parking lot.

Of course, most performance measures are the result of a number of pieces of information, all combined into one calculated result. It is important, therefore, that the data collection process take into account the involuntary dissolution of validity that can occur from the mixing of inputs from various time periods. I've seen incredible conclusions reached when the reported performance measurement was calculated from mixed-period data.

One example is a well-known rapid transit system that was controlled by a process that calculated how fast a train should go according to a prediction model rather than actual position measurements. In other words, where the car was, at a particular moment, wasn't considered when the throttle or the brake was commanded. The first tests of that strategy resulted in the train running right through the blockade at the end of a long run. Accumulated errors that occurred because of a lack of synchronizing location with time caused a disastrous result.

The sample system that captures data should be well designed to assure that data collections represent an accurate time-slice of compatible information (Exhibit 5.3).

Time-slicing should obviously also report the precise time of an event such that the record of historical data takes on

**Exhibit 5.3**   Detailed Time-History of Cost Components

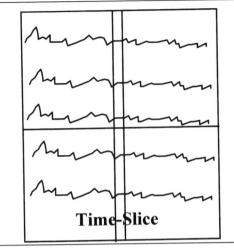

**Time-Slice**

matrix configurations with the sample times on one coordinate and the data values on the other (Exhibit 5.4).

Therefore, a historical database with a time-history created from time-sliced information becomes the foundation for harvesting the intrinsic value from performance measurements. The ability to correlate events, see cause and effect, and calculate the relationship between events will be possible when you have the ability to tie measurements together with *time*. It also permits the "identification of the source of the problem." A time-history becomes the archive of information

**Exhibit 5.4**   A Time-Slice Analysis

| Time | Cases | Data | | | | |
|------|-------|---|---|---|---|---|
| 0840 | 6.2 | ∼ | ∼ | ∼ | ∼ | ∼ |
| 0920 | 6.6 | ∼ | ∼ | ∼ | ∼ | ∼ |
| 1005 | 7.1 | ∼ | ∼ | ∼ | ∼ | ∼ |
| 1055 | 6.6 | ∼ | ∼ | ∼ | ∼ | ∼ |
| 1145 | 6.8 | ∼ | ∼ | ∼ | ∼ | ∼ |

that permits us to study "what if" and "next time" scenarios. Those data can also be used to recalculate performance measures and cost, simply by scrolling backwards and forwards through the database.

## CHAPTER 5 HIGHLIGHTS:

A. Learning from the journey.

B. Messages from performance behavior.

C. Importance of data presentation methods.

D. Necessity of data integrity.

E. Benefit of correlations analysis.

# CHAPTER 6

# Use of Costs in a Business Strategy

Remember our premise: we make and sell multiple products to multiple clients. Given that environment, do we know where we generate the most profit and what could be done to improve on that position? What is a *business strategy* and do we need one?

I'm a believer in "Plan your work and work your plan" (IBM gave us that platitude years ago!). It does imply focus and elimination of waste. That kind of thought process is hard to dismiss as trivial. I believe that every business was originally conceived with the idea of making a profit. That basic concept creates a need for some form of a business plan in order to turn ideas and efforts into profits. Every designer and engineer needs to know how much thruput, design volume, or rated thruput is intended. These fundamental criteria set the basis for the planning process and reflect on the ability of the basis of the original design to generate a profit. The design plan is always the foundation for the business case and determines whether or not a manufacturing facility should be built. Unfortunately, conditions never stay the same, so it is difficult to achieve the profit plan month by month. Nevertheless, the business plan is always to keep costs lower than revenue, or the facility would never exist in the first place.

What are some of the events that disengage a business from its plan to make a profit? Costs are invariably one of the factors. You have heard the old saying that "two things are sure in life: death and taxes." There is one other "sure thing": costs never go down; they only go up. They don't even stand still. They are slippery, mobile, evasive things—those costs. The other side of the equation is revenue. I can look at a single product and study its ability to generate revenue. When I do, I make some revealing discoveries: (a) I may be selling that single product for several different prices; and (b) each deal has its own merit (or basis). Sometimes the size of the order provokes preferential discounts. Perhaps, the order is considered to be "incremental" at the time and special considerations were made because of the unexpected, extended volume. Sometime an investment is made to gain market share. Other times salespeople's reports of what the competition is doing affect prices. (I've wondered how these factors would change if salespeople were evaluated on their contribution to profit, instead of volume.)

The breakaway of actual performance from the prediction in the business plan occurs for many reasons. The challenge for the managers of the business is to know where they are and how to steer their way toward an acceptable level of financial performance. What are the ingredients necessary for any business to succeed? We have already presented the answer: "you can't manage profit if you can't measure cost." Knowledge of cost, in a time frame that permits corrective action, is a necessary ingredient in any successful business strategy.

Given the ability to measure costs using the techniques I've already described and combining them with the sales/orders (selling price) provides the basis for that important performance measure: *profit*.

We've already discussed the change or dynamics of the profit measurement. Now we need to determine how to gain value toward the goal of our business plan from this new, calculated business performance variable.

Because profit is what is left over between selling price and cost, we need to understand where each is headed and why. We can go to our sales and marketing people for forecasts. We can buy advice from the outside world. But we can learn much from a time-history, a great tool for seeing just where cost has been and for understanding why.

I had a semiconductor manufacturing client whose products' selling price demonstrated a predictable life cycle. At introduction, selling price was at peak, and as volumes (and competitive pressures) increased, the prices began their journey downward.

Now it was clear to everyone that the market price decayed, but few were conscious of how quickly and of the impact of that decay on profit. Obviously, pressures and efficiencies contributed to cost improvements. When we begin to plot cost on that same curve (Exhibit 6.1), we see the profit margin erode.

This simple approach to tracking the life cycle of profit allows the business strategist to make decisions about how (and how much) to negotiate and/or when to make the decision to drop a product from the line. Knowledge of the trend of both cost and selling price is seldom studied at the detailed, product level, yet it holds the key to success.

Given that we can have an integrated system that will give us these measurements, by product, how can we use this information in our business strategy?

**Exhibit 6.1**  The Cost Behavior Curve

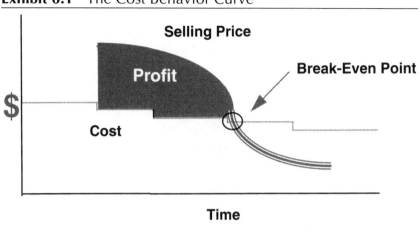

These measurements permit, even encourage, control of manufacturing costs and overhead. With a knowledge of where and in what direction they are going, the cause and opportunity for lowering costs can be determined. The presence of a baseline on cost, updated frequently, will drive appropriate behavior, especially when innovative management teams link incentives to that appropriate behavior.

Production planners and product line managers can also use this kind of information to identify the minimum order (production run) size. Remember our discussion about the variability of unit cost based on run length? Planners can actually forecast profit contribution for a production schedule, using historical algorithms developed from measured cost and production history (another reason for the time-stamped history).

Your marketing group may learn to anticipate volumetric gains in profit margin and focus/promote clients who buy larger orders less frequently. Some may study various scenarios of how the sum of the contributions to margin change when the product mix or the promotions of certain products in certain territories change. Certainly, knowledge is enhanced when some history of profitability by product is understood.

Activity-based costing creates models of each activity within the business. Certainly, the balance and utilization of each activity versus the others are factors, but as a planning tool, that knowledge permits accurate estimates of the cost of new products. The accuracy of the business case for the introduction of new products is dramatically enhanced by the use of this kind of measured information.

Operations will discover their manufacturing limits of profitable operation. The measurement of minimum order size and correlation of profit to run length is only one area in which operations can gain. The measurement and costing of rework activities such as quality adjustment (the cost of not getting it right the first time) or of recycle streams to keep quality acceptable can reveal significant information about where costs are being consumed. Smart production managers soon learn which of these measures are significant enough to focus on. The 80/20 rule certainly applies here.

One of the most revealing uses of this measurement is the configuration and distribution of costs within specific orders (i.e., by customers). Can you imagine being exposed to the knowledge of how much profit you gained from each customer? Let me reveal to you a few of the surprises I've found in the past several years:

- My largest customer yields the least profit.
- Some of my customers are actually causing me to lose money.
- It's clear now that I make some profit and then I give it away.
- Some of my customers are clearly smart enough to have bought only my losers.
- If I had only known I crossed the break-even point, I wouldn't have been selling at a loss.

The business strategy clearly can benefit from improved knowledge of cost. The availability of detailed histories of cost, broken down in modules measuring each source, is invaluable in the diagnosis of where the priorities for improvement should be focused. The actions you have to take to be a success in business begin with a knowledge of the price tag attached to each. The manager is then confronted with facts on which he or she can base the business strategy, instead of solely on intuition and experience.

## CHAPTER 6 HIGHLIGHTS:

A. Main goal is to make a profit.

B. All businesses conceived with profit as a goal.

C. Variations in cost and revenue impact profits.

D. Measurements necessary for control.

E. Knowledge tells where profit comes from.

F. Diagnosis as a finite science, rather than a guessing game.

G. Stronger and easier business strategy implemented with good cost data.

# CHAPTER 7

# Strategic Benefits

Many issues confront the business strategist:

- What products should I be producing for these market conditions?
- Where should I improve to achieve the biggest gain?
- What is my cost of excess quality?
- What is my profit margin? By product? By market?

The challenge of finding the path to profitability starts with the business plan but is won or lost with the playing of the game. The winners always seem to have some edge. Do they know more than the others, or are they just lucky? The availability of factual performance information in time to plan a course of profitable behavior is an advantage every manager dreams of.

Literal measurement of costs, on a frequent basis, can provide numerous benefits to the strategic business planner. Historical results, with their apparent dynamic trends, can be used to show details about where costs are consumed. The time-histories of individual cost elements include information on magnitude, variability, relationship to cost drivers, and prioritization of need for improvements.

Measured costs and their variability by order size can play a strategic role in product pricing decisions. Fundamental knowledge of how costs behave seasonally, by change in production run size, and with different degrees of quality and special requests by customers can make a tremendous difference in the market strategy. Most organizations simply base market strategy on planned profitability, and the sales force accepts all kinds of variants to gain an order, without any knowledge of the cost consequence. ABC measurements can give you the actual cost behavior of every variant you can throw at it, allowing you the benefit of pricing those deviations in a way to cover your costs. (You may choose to buy a piece of business, but you can, at least, make that decision based on facts.)

One of the most strategic actions a manager takes is to decide what went wrong and how to correct that fault. We've already seen how knowledge of cost consumption and behavior can be learned from this source of calculation.

We stated earlier that the most benefits to be derived would be for those who made multiple products and sold them to many different clients. At any given point in time, different products will have different profit margin contributions—some because of their different consumption of cost activities, some because of their different production run sizes, and some because of the special requests that often carry cost consequences. The decisions about product mix may be purely driven by orders now, but think of the strategic benefit of knowing that certain products can yield better margins than others and making overruns and inventory in the excess may greatly offset the cost of carrying that inventory. Profit enhancement strategies may be built around profit-by-product knowledge in a number of ways:

- Make to inventory versus make to order—maximize profit potential through longer, more efficient production runs

- Better discounts—knowing when opportunity exists

- Minimum order sizes

- Charges for special orders

- Profit forecasts at time of product in schedule

These opportunities all tell us that cost knowledge can enhance our bottom line if we use the information to make strategic product mix decisions.

Cost information can certainly be a strategic measurement for individual or organizational accountability. Most performance objectives today are built around sales or production volume. The enterprise model in Exhibit 7.1 calls attention to many business processes that should be accountable for a

**Exhibit 7.1** Value Chain

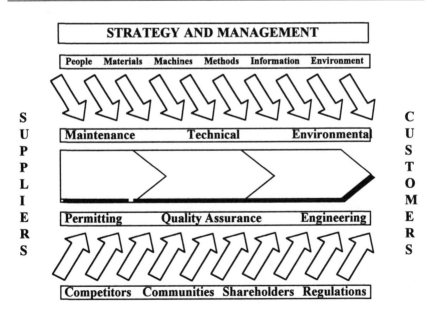

winning performance level. A company needs performance measurements to drive behavior that generates the most profit. Wouldn't you rather have an actual profit meter for measuring the performance and various manufacturing and business processes that comprise your company?

ABC measurements are being used today by many organizations to drive appropriate behavior and as the basis for carefully designed incentive programs that combine volume and profitability as accountability measures that keep the business in good health.

Deming's philosophy of quality and continuous improvement has permeated our business management strategies for several years. Recent studies have shown that organization changes tend to decay back to their original performance (Hawthorne effect) if they are not sustained by some "cultural incentive mechanism" (measurements) (Exhibit 7.2).

Remember: measurements drive behavior. They always have and they always will. The precise measurement of the

**Exhibit 7.2** The Improvement Trend

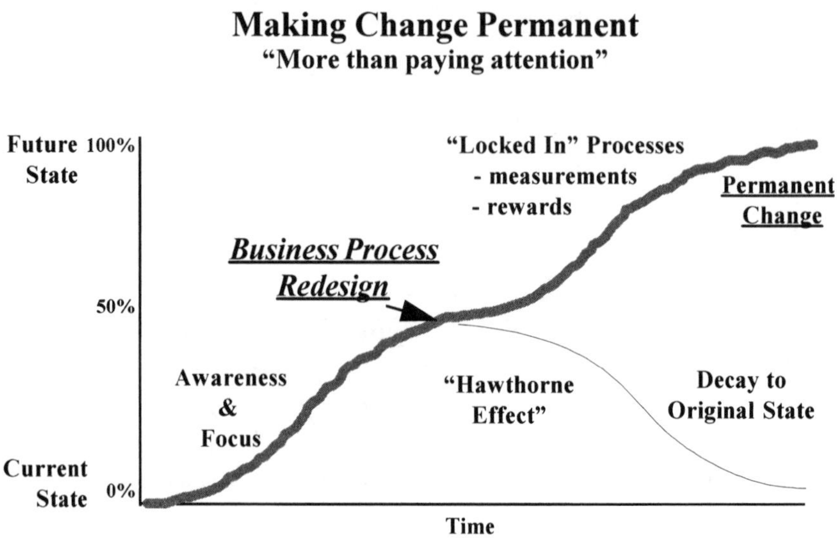
Making Change Permanent
"More than paying attention"
Future State
100%
50%
Current State
0%
"Locked In" Processes
- measurements
- rewards
Permanent Change
Business Process Redesign
Awareness & Focus
"Hawthorne Effect"
Decay to Original State
Time

cost of various business and manufacturing processes is the most fundamental of business performance measures. ABC is *not* a new cost accounting system. It is a strategic planning tool.

## CHAPTER 7 HIGHLIGHTS:

A. Using historical behavior to establish a strategy.

B. Planning at a detailed level.

C. Learning from cause and effect.

D. Setting profit enhancement strategies.

E. Strategy forms the basis for the operating plan.

F. Making improvements permanent with measurements.

# CHAPTER 8

# Tactical Benefits

Every hour of every day, managers are making some change to a process. Perhaps they increase the production rate or make adjustments to improve the quality. Some might be trying to achieve a level of predictable performance. Other managers may worry that these changes may have a cost consequence, but not the operator. He or she has neither seen any information on cost nor ever been held accountable for cost.

We've discussed in earlier chapters how some cost drivers are actual process flows or production rates. An activity-based costing system can utilize hours and rates to calculate this new piece of information (cost) in such a short time frame that it can actually be played back to the operator as a feedback measurement of profit.

Workers in operations have never seen this before and will have to be educated about what to expect, what it means, and how to use it. But this application of real-time cost information can have extraordinary tactical value in a manufacturing operation. Let's look at some of the questions real-time cost measures might answer:

- Is my manufacturing process running profitably right now?

- What specific production issues impact my profitability the most?

- What is the sensitivity to cost when I change procedures?

- What is my minimum volume to break even?

- Do I actually make money some days and lose it on others? Why?

Cost information, in time to be used for corrective and appropriate actions, is highly tactical in that it allows proactive behavior. Having information that helps direct the process to the best possible performance is the pinnacle of a performance measurement instrument.

Cost data can be presented to operations and factory floor personnel in a variety of ways. You seldom need to enumerate the absolute value of a calculated cost to gain appropriate behavior. You may choose to show the actual numeric value or you might choose a performance scale (1 to 100) or a "green is good, red is bad" color code. Your imagination can create a variety of ways to tell operators that they just did something that made the cost go down (or up). I've spent many hours in control rooms and on factory floors. Operators there get to know their processes in great detail. Give them this new form of meaningful information (and perhaps some way to earn an incentive from improved performance) and they will amaze you with their knowledge of process behavior. They will adjust and tune that old process to make that profit meter almost *sing* for you. They get competitive too. Watch the shifts compete with each other once they have this new form of process performance measurement.

(I have one client who gave his operators a bonus based on improved profitability—to a cap of $250 per month. His investment in this new measurement system was paid for in two months. Measurements did drive behavior!)

A feedback display of cost information allows operators to see the impact of changes they make immediately. They no longer have to wait for someone to tell them if that decision was good or bad; now they receive real-time decision support. The quality of operating decisions will benefit from this form of measurement.

Production planners have always tried to get orders filled; that is their basic objective. Business demands have increasingly added a new dimension to that objective—at the lowest cost. However, the cost targets were intuitive and imperfect. They were also indirectly accounted for, using associated measurements such as consumption of raw materials, yield, and labor hours. Real-time cost management can provide measures to such detail that one can actually read the break-even point on contribution to margin, making it possible to mark the minimum order size for future production schedule development. There is no sense in scheduling small orders that lose money unless they can be combined—with marketing/sales consent, of course. But let's take advantage of this knowledge.

Feedback of cost activities can be a significant tool for cost avoidance. Suddenly, a measurement can tell you the cost consequence of a tool that is getting dull or of a fouled heat-exchanger. Many small events happen every day in manufacturing areas. But continuing the process to meet a deadline is sometimes a poor decision. With real-time feedback of costs, your decision can be based on economics (after safety, of course).

The use of cost information as a process control variable is new. Technology allows us to combine the sources of data and measures necessary to calculate the dollar value of our process. Why not use that information to enable our people to make smart business decisions? They will be able to get realistic indications of how well they are doing, in the dollar terms that everyone understands. After all, money is the universal language.

## CHAPTER 8 HIGHLIGHTS:

    A. How cost information can be obtained quickly.

    B. Tactical questions that need answers.

    C. Various ways to present cost information.

    D. Value in workers' knowledge of the process.

    E. Correlation of cause and effect.

    F. Minimum order size.

    G. Proactive cost management.

    H. A new process control variable: cost.

# CHAPTER 9

# Executive Uses of Activity-Based Management

This book is about managing profit; that is, learning how to understand the components of the business and how each of them impacts the bottom line. The two major categories of profit are *revenue* and *cost*. Our focus is on the operating/manufacturing side: *cost*.

As an executive, you have the responsibility to see that your enterprise generates enough income to perpetuate the normal upkeep and growth of the business and reward the investment of the shareholders. Those basic ingredients ensure the longevity of the enterprise. It seems such an easy task when everything is going well. The question is always: *Can it be better?* In the mind of every executive is the nagging idea that there are ways to improve the performance of the business.

Years have been spent on improving departmental quality and squeezing more production out of the same equipment or staff. Many good efforts have been made, only to discover from the subsequent financial reports that forecasts still fail to be met and no one can really explain why.

The enterprise may be too big and complex to understand all its facets. The variances from the forecasts may seem hopelessly lost in excuses and cloudy explanations that don't really connect to direct causes, and you may lack good, absolute directives to correct the problems and steer the enterprise in a tight direction toward improved profitability.

We have all suffered through those monthly meetings, trying to understand where the profits eroded. It doesn't have to be such a mystery. By breaking the enterprise down into its fundamental processes and treating each process as a small business (at least by measuring and understanding how it consumes cost), we can blow away some of the clouds of smoke shrouding the mystery of why profits occur and why they do not.

I have already described the use of costs in a business strategy, but this leads into more questions about how you, the executive, can understand performance and the degree of improvement of each of these business processes. In addition, there are opportunities to use this activity-based management (ABM) technique to manage the financial performance of specific decisions that you make, in such areas as product slate, customer management, and the discovery of just how well certain investments really impacted the areas in which you put new money. It is in these categories that the true value of ABM begins to enable the executive to be *in control* of what is important to the longevity of the business: *profit*.

*You can't manage profit, if you can't measure cost.*

This book provides a framework, an architecture, for the ABM performance history database that will become the reservoir of knowledge from which you can make decisions (see Chapter 15—Harvesting the Value from ABC). Here we focus on some of the high-value uses of ABM information, building on the value pyramid concept (Exhibit 9.1).

You can use the pyramid to condense, analyze, and draw conclusions that will lead you to the knowledge of how to manage the problem under study.

We will spend some time discussing areas of decision support that will enable the executive to better control the bottom line of the enterprise. Recognize that it is essential that the data generated and fed into the decision support database be based on the actual measurement of each activity in that process.

This is so important that I'm going to reiterate the steps as follows:

1. Take a process view of the enterprise

2. Break down each process into activities

3. Understanding what is consumed in each activity

   • Resources (labor, maintenance, SG&A)

   • Asset costs

   • Raw materials

   • Energy

**Exhibit 9.1**   Value Pyramid

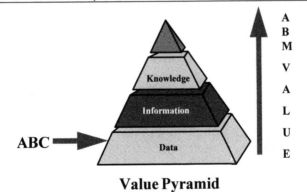

Value Pyramid

4. Identify ways to measure and cost each consumable

5. Relate everything in terms of cost of product

These are the basic activity-based costing principles.

But raw cost measurement data represent only the foundation for executive knowledge. Somehow, we have to transform those data into something more useful. I call the complete solution Activity Based Management. Its components are

1. ABC model(s) for raw cost measurement

2. Database of cost performance history

3. Decision support applications

Decision support application needs to be defined. Separate applications can be prepared to analyze and support decisions for specific purposes. I have used ABM knowledge to manage the following five categories:

- Cost tracking
- Product line management
- Customer profitability management
- Investment performance tracking
- Improvement project measurement

These categories represent only a general set of decision support applications understood today. I am certain that time will reveal many more.

## COST TRACKING

The first surprise that is usually encountered when activity-based costs are seen is the relative magnitude of the costs in individual areas. The knowledge that labor or machine time (production rate) or perhaps off-spec production is your major cost consumer can sometimes be new knowledge to you and your organization. A Pareto diagram identifying cost activities and drivers from largest to smallest will prioritize your efforts in cost management and will keep you focused on putting your efforts where they will get the most return for your investment.

By understanding that an activity-based model calculates the cost of quantities of all types of consumables, you quickly capture the need to be careful in the design of the time period of each data set sent to the activity-based model. A time period most commonly used by the financial group is by quarter. The reason was that the quarter corresponded to the frequency of *closing the books,* simply because that was the schedule that the accounting department followed.

Time-period selection (remember, I advocate actual measurements for as many cost drivers as can be implemented) can dramatically enhance the value of cost information. If the data-collection period is still the quarter, many of the costs associated with that period will simply be summaries of spending, nonspecific to the subjects of interest: *products.* But if you will select time periods that correspond to production runs of individual products, you will capture the specific costs of that product at that point in time. Remember this is only a snapshot of cost behavior.

My wife is a great family historian. She has snapshots of people and events going back several generations. It is fun to look back and see how things were "back then." This concept applied to business means that if we capture enough "snapshots" of cost behavior and log pertinent performance information about that set of performance calculations, then we can begin to develop a model of how each activity behaves. Remember, in Chapter 1, my confession that the behavior of the refinery unit was nonlinear; that is, there was a peak in profit contribution long before maximum thruput was achieved. The point is that many time periods are better than a few, when trying to understand the cost behavior of our enterprise. We need to select time periods that will correlate with the way we schedule and run our manufacturing operations and then we will have a database of information that can be transformed into knowledge, such as

1. Overall profitability of single products
2. Predictability of product profitability
3. Variance of profitability from one line to another
4. Seasonal variations
5. Impact of run length on profitability

Another significant use of a well-designed and populated database is *diagnosis.* How many times have you asked yourself, "I wonder what that cost me?" If you keep the costs of each activity and time-stamp, archive, and database them, you have the ability to go back and diagnose where the excursions occurred. You can literally plot time trends of individual activity costs and you might discover that some slight change in overall cost was due to a major event in one single activity—an unreported event—but you have the cost history. You might also see that some costs are out of control—that is, they vary two to ten times across your samples and there is no rationale as to why. Plugging small leaks is a good practice—the ability to find them is now at hand.

## PRODUCT LINE MANAGEMENT

How well do you understand the profitability of each product in your list of deliverables? Do you know if one product really makes a lot of money and why? If I were to ask different people in the organization which products were best to make, would their answers correlate with the most profitable products the sales and production scheduling people planned to produce? Does the organization know that different production levels of different products can move the profit contribution up and down the scale? Are they operating from knowledge or from market demand alone? How strategic is product mix?

I have seen cases of downsizing and product-line rationalization (in other words, close-out) resulting in lower volume but higher profits, in situations in which some products actually gave away profits—their costs being greater than their revenue. In fact I have yet to implement ABM in *any* manufacturing facility in which I haven't found circumstances of unprofitable products. Many situations dictate the profitability of a product, but they need to be understood! I've seen too many cases of "good" products generating profit and "bad" ones eroding that profit away, with everyone unconcerned at the end of the day.

It is imperative to construct the cost data history by product and by any other subcategory as appropriate, so you can understand what trends product costs and profitability are taking. Life cycles become real, and events that might go unnoticed that impact the bottom line suddenly jump to the attention of those who can do something about them. Imagine having a product line management function with accountability for profit contribution. Pretty revolutionary, isn't it? How about holding the production scheduling group accountable for a profit contribution target for each week's schedule? If you know historical profit contribution by product (and associated production variables), you should be able to forecast the hypothetical profitability of a schedule before it is run. *And* if you really want to see the value of this information, use it with an optimization model that can maximize the profit contribution of a production line or facility. Constraints from inventory, sales, machine limits, and so on will cap this effort, but no manual schedule ever comes close to the performance of a good optimization model, fed with real cost-performance data. Try some of these ideas for using ABM cost data to get to know your products better. You may discover you like some better than others, for reasons you never understood before.

## CUSTOMER PROFITABILITY MANAGEMENT

After you gain a good knowledge of which products make profit and under what circumstances, you have the ability to combine sales by customer information and to see profit by customer and, perhaps, if you select time periods well, by customer order as well. You should be able to gain knowledge about your business with each client that will enable you to better manage that relationship.

Customers fall into three categories:

1. Those who buy your product on price alone
2. Those who buy because of your service and price
3. Those who don't know why they buy

There used to be a lot of customers who didn't know why they bought what they did, but not anymore. Customers are getting smarter and smarter. They will work you against other suppliers, and they will smile while doing it; after all, they're in business too. I learned long ago that the first rule of negotiation was to know your thresholds. You have to have knowledge in a tough negotiation if you want to be a winner on the bottom line. It's easy to win an order by cutting price, but knowing how far you can go is dependent on sound knowledge of specific cost information. ABM can provide you with the analysis you need to learn which customers are thoroughly knowledgeable about the comparative prices of similar products from several suppliers and is "shopping you" for the best prices, buying a product slate from you that might be made up of your lowest profit margins.

You can use this knowledge to improve the strategy of what mix of products you sell to a client—using knowledge to better manage your client portfolio. If you categorize your clients by their contribution to your profits, rather than only by the volume they buy, you will be able to see your clients in a way not previously available, that is, in the order of their importance to your bottom line. It is rare for us to really understand how important a customer is. We generally like the customer for the volume purchased from us, but I've seen numerous cases in which the *big 6* or the *top 10* customers contribute little or nothing to the bottom line. They achieve discounts, favors (albeit expensive ones), best pricing, sometimes even forced deals (that is, I'll only buy product "S" if you sell me product "B" at this price).

The real question is, "Do you know the profitability of a customer's business?" The second question then becomes, "If you did, what could you do about it?" I can think of about a dozen things I'd do, but this book is about how to find out if a customer's business is profitable, not how to manage customers.

ABM data can be invaluable in tracking the historical behavior of clients. You really do need to know if your customer is good for your business.

## INVESTMENT PERFORMANCE TRACKING

I have seen hundreds of AFEs (Authorization for Expenditure) that promised 16% to 25% ROI. If every one of these really delivered what it promised, then why isn't our overall financial performance better than the 5% to 10% average of American manufacturers? I can't believe that we let ourselves get fooled by these claims of performance that history tells us can't possibly be true; yet we make enormous investment decisions every day on the basis of these forecasts and promises.

I am going to suggest that as you design your activity-based management philosophy, that you adopt a *business process model* premise into the AFE process as well. If you can align the definition of which business processes will be impacted by an investment, then the ABM models (remember processes consist of activities and tasks) can help you measure the performance, over time, of those processes supposedly impacted. Can you honestly say that you know if the return on investments for even your large projects was really achieved?

Alignment of AFE investments with the enterprise model used in ABM will enable specific baseline and time-history behavior to be recorded, documented, and used to track investment performance. Of course, numerous caveats and categories of investments have to be considered in that analysis, but you can be certain of one thing: when the parties seeking approval of investment funds know that their project is going to be measured, their promises are going to be a lot more sound. This is especially true if their own personal performance measures are somehow tied to their accuracy in forecasting the benefits of major investments. I believe accountability is good, and I believe that supporting accountability with consistent, defensible information is essential. ABM can provide that. Consider using a separate investment performance tracking application to use ABM data as a source for managing your corporate investments in the future of your business.

## IMPROVEMENT PROJECT MEASUREMENT

Deming introduced the concept of *continuous improvement,* and we often have a slate of ongoing projects to accomplish changes in the performance of bits and pieces of our business. How did he choose those improvement projects and on what basis will we judge their success?

I see many efforts initiated simply on the basis of "a good story . . . sounds logical to me." How easy it is to launch a series of small innocent efforts that make little or no real improvement in the performance of the business.

Isn't the bottom line one of our most important issues? Certainly, operability, quality, people issues, and other factors must be part of the equation, but the cost and benefit of every investment must somehow be considered and that is what I am discussing. ABM can be the platform for extracting the "real" cost of an effort. I can also trend the change in behavior of a task, an activity, or a process at a level of detail to know, beyond the shadow of a doubt, if an effort to make some improvement is actually achieving its goal.

How do you select those areas to improve? Do you have a method that helps you set priorities on what will benefit your business the most? ABM history will allow you to see where you have the biggest problems in managing both the level and the magnitude of cost. Look for trends, variations, and size of expense items in the detail breakdown of the ABM cost data. You will find the information you need to decide where to make changes. The basis for selection should be focused on how big the problem is and how much impact your effort will have. A balance between magnitude and strategic importance is dictated and you need all the information you can get to make a knowledgeable decision.

Improvement projects are generally focused on a process. The concepts of ABC measurement can be applied to demonstrate change in the same way as you would measure the changes to several processes impacted by a large investment.

The executive has many opportunities to be smarter about the way business behavior changes by taking advantage of ABM techniques. The basic construction of ABM models provides the foundation for knowledge-based decision support. The decision-support applications defined in this chapter are but the tip of the iceberg of ways to use this information for the improvement of your business performance.

## CHAPTER 9 HIGHLIGHTS:

A. Impossibility of managing profit without measuring cost.

B. Historical difficulty of explaining cost variance.

C. Reiteration of ABM principles.

D. Cost tracking—production performance.

E. Product line management.

F. Customer profitability management.

G. Investment performance tracking.

H. Improvement project measurement.

# CHAPTER 10

# A New Look at Business

Without exception, my clients have always been dubious about activity-based cost data the first time they see it because it is always different from the numbers they have worked with in the past. We tend to accept known quantities and to reject or be defensive about things that are different. How do you gain credibility for the newly calculated measurements that your activity models have generated? Several factors relating to the way you look at the business and how you present the information are important. This positioning is crucial to the acceptance of the information contained in the results.

First, the *design* and *identification* of the cost elements themselves must be facilitated with and confirmed by those who will ultimately be impacted by the results. That is, people must assume ownership of the design of the cost models. Once they agree to the elements of cost and to what makes them vary, they have accepted the concept of measurement-driven, activity-based cost calculation. From that point forward, the results are theirs, not yours, and you only have to learn how to appropriately segregate and present information to assist the various users in making appropriate decisions about their portion of the business.

Chapter 12 discusses the design and architecture of the database and its specific elements, to aid in the design of the system itself. This chapter is concerned with elements of the cost themselves. It is important to recognize the many ways that you can look at cost and even more importantly, the many different ways your users will want to look at their costs. I can't reinforce enough the need to be prepared for the reaction: "But, this isn't what I was expecting." There are always special considerations, significant events, unplanned events that operations will say are "never going to happen again," and a host of other influences that will alter the steady state that manufacturers would prefer to be used as a measure. The reality is that actual is actual. Business decisions may override actual results, but they will never alter the fact that those results occurred. What is helpful is to have had the foresight to capture data in a sequence of smaller time periods (and to calculate, by computer of course, the cost results for each of those smaller time periods) so that performance can be tracked, trended, and correlated to those special events that are being used as excuses to discount the results of cost and profit measurement.

Once the cost models are constructed, it's time to move on and learn how to get better value from this information. Discovering how to capture data and to use the results is as big a challenge as the actual design and construction of the cost models themselves. So, you are not finished when the model output is completed. All you've done is assemble the basic data. You still have to transform it into information and then into knowledge. Your executive decision support applications will be the building blocks that will take you across the goal line in this game of improved profitability.

One of the first data capture basics that you must focus on is the period for which you are going to make a cost calculation. Ask yourself what periods of time are important to the decisions you must make to manage this business. Let me suggest a few:

1. Choose time periods over which you have some control and that correlate to defined components of your business (products, customers, production runs, etc.).

2. Time periods don't all have to be the same, similar, or equal segments (shift, day, week, month); they can be irregular and intermixed. Remember, the computer should be measuring *cost drivers* and calculating the consumptions of material and resources associated with this cost element.

3. Consider using production schedules as planned periods, but try to trigger each event's start and finish by some activity within the production control system.

   (*Note:* Be sure you take scrap and recycle into consideration in your cost models. "Finished product" is not an accurate basis for dollars consumed, only for that amount of product that must bear the total cost.)

The period or *heartbeat* frequency of your manufacturing cycle should be the ultimate goal for the model to produce intermediate results. Now, I will caution you that only a portion of the cost elements will vary during one of these periods.

For example, taxes don't change dynamically, but consumption of energy, raw material conversion efficiency, and labor components will.

Don't be afraid to recalculate on a frequent or random sample basis. You will begin to isolate those cost elements that really influence change in manufactured cost and you will begin to see how much variation actually exists in the consumption of cost. (Chapter 4 discusses the dynamics of real-time data.)

The secret of getting value from cost data is learning how to correlate cause and effect. This puts you in control of your costs and helps to identify opportunities for improvement in the performance of each element of cost.

Imagine that you have chosen events to mark your data samples that correlate to transition interfaces between products. You are segmenting data capture so you can identify the cost of each product. You will have some very useful information. You will see the impact of product manufacturing difficulty. No manufacturing process can be optimal for every variety of product that is made. *And* you will discover that many factors influence the cost of the same product made on the same production line, from day to day, week to week, and season to season. Yes, factors such as what product you made just before this one, run length, group of shift operators, weather quality of raw materials—a thousand different factors can make a huge difference in the performance (and thus the cost) of a manufacturing process. Selection of an appropriate period of data collection can support this level of knowledge or, conversely, longer period selections (monthly or quarterly) can suppress or average out the dynamic that might enable you to take advantage of a better strategy or decision that could save you money.

Indeed, knowledge *is* power!

Once you have begun to collect data on cost of production by product, it is important to archive that knowledge along with the appropriate data that can be used in subsequent evaluation and analysis. Such data include:

1. Which production line
2. Run length

3. Abnormal events associated with a particular run

4. Ambient conditions

5. Upstream events and quality of new materials

Although you may not be able to capture all of this information, these types of clues will correlate to the behavior of cost and can be influential in your management decisions for improvement projects—especially when you understand how much they influence your financial performance.

Once you have a complete historical time line of production cost performance, you have the opportunity to cross-reference sales information. You should be able to make some good judgments about which production runs were shipped to which customer and for what price. This marriage of the order fulfillment information with the cost data should take place in the data repository, never in the cost model. You have a great deal more flexibility when you build the merger of "what goes to whom" into a separate application; the cost models will be complex enough by themselves.

This combination of information will give you some very useful knowledge. You will be able to see profit (selling price less cost) by customer and by order component. Then by combining the profit behavior of each product purchased by a single customer, you can compile composite profitability of doing business with an individual customer. I'm going to predict that some surprises are in store for you. Your *very best* customers (by whatever standard you now measure them) will change position in your mind, once you shift to a basis of how each of them contributes to your profitability.

Remember, customers are in business, too, and they are always shopping for the best deal they can get. They may be shopping you for those products with less margin and buying more of them. After all, that's what you would do. Now, you want to be smarter than they are, and an intimate knowledge of your costs, updated frequently, can enable your customer management team to make better decisions than ever before.

This information is also of extraordinary value to product management and product development groups. I can't imagine not knowing specific information about how much it actually is costing to manufacture the products for which I am clearly responsible. Without this knowledge, I would have planned and forecasted a manufacturing cost and would be anxiously awaiting true and current tracking of the actual measurements to compare with my forecast.

The cause and effect correlations alluded to earlier certainly have enormous influence on this type of function and accountability.

The previous chapter listed and discussed several decision support applications:

- Cost tracking
- Product line management
- Customer profitability management
- Investment performance tracking
- Improvement project measurement

I have attempted to stress the importance of how you choose to look at the data on these types of accountabilities within your management structure. The form of presentation is often trivialized in the planning process. I strongly urge you to take care in designing the presentation of this type of information. Remember that managers are looking for indicators, trends, responses to actions previously taken, as well as many obscure pieces of information that you can never incorporate into a routine report. Graphical techniques should be used to present this information. These can be trend charts and plots of comparative performance. I use Pareto charts and bar charts (see Appendix B) to look at product and customer relative profitabilities. I use trend charts to follow the behavior of product costs and customer profitabilities, looking for deviations from the expected. Overlays of target behaviors are always excellent additions for goal comparisons or performance measurements.

You will find many ways to present these types of data, and you will be requested to present the information in many different contexts. It is important to find a graphics capability that is easy to configure and alter as conditions change.

## CHAPTER 10 HIGHLIGHTS:

A. Acceptance through ownership.

B. Anticipation of resistance.

C. Critical nature of data collection period.

D. Enabling cause and effect.

E. Product and customer profitability management.

F. Presentation techniques.

# CHAPTER 11

# Good Business/Bad Business

All salespeople will tell you that any business is good business. Their whole life is built around the concept of gathering in every single order that they can capture, within the rules and limits of negotiation that constrain them. They will work at cross-purposes with your desire to maximize profit by attempting to make the product as "price attractive" as you will permit. They probably don't even know what parameters of the sale (special handling, quick delivery, split shipments, nonstandard specification adjustments, and many more) affect the cost, and by how much. In other words, salespeople believe that volume is all-important and they will fight anyone who attempts to curtail their ability to garner every little piece they hope to add to their accounts.

Obviously, these hypothetical salespeople are driven by the classic measure: volume. This might be different if you had reached the point of being able to support their ability to know the profit margin of every order they negotiate and if you have changed the rules to measure and reward them on their contribution to profit. They will be quick to adapt to the new incentive plan. In fact, when you first develop the ABM system and begin to deploy it in value-generating ways across the enterprise, you will be surprised to discover that your top volume-generating salespeople are not your top profit-generating individuals (Exhibit 11.1).

In the new scenario, you empower salespeople (that is, you give them both information and authority) to negotiate in behalf of securing good business for the company. You make them part of the profit-generating team, and they know that they have a major role in helping to manage the revenue side of the profit equation in such a way that they protect the business from being a bad business. They have increased self-confidence, knowing that they now have enough information to see how their work affects the success or failure of the business. Now they *are* connected to the bottom line.

**Exhibit 11.1**   Contribution by Salesperson

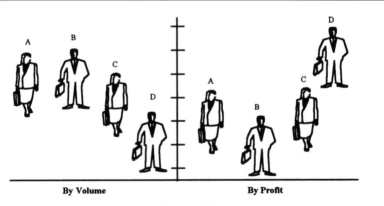

By Volume                                    By Profit

Contribution by Salesman

Your sales and marketing groups can now begin to add a new dimension to their planning and forecasting efforts. They can now begin to focus in on how to match your manufacturing group's profit-generating capabilities to the market opportunities in such a way as to improve the contribution to margin. Once they know profit by product and the parameters that impact those performances, they can strategically focus on how to manage product line production in such a way as to improve the performance of profit. Some products may be dropped, some may be modified, and some may be promoted for increased volume.

A business plan is designed to create the direction for a company to follow in order to create profits. Many factors that you could use will be available through the use of ABM. The factors include:

- Size of order
- Variance from standards
- Nonstandard delivery
- Give-away price

I can't tell how many times I've asked to see the business plan and have discovered that no one knows where profit is generated or how to take control in a strategy of promoting those products that make the most money. Nor is it understood which markets and customers are profit's best friends. With ABM as a tool, you can become the victor in the good business/bad business battle.

Much of this book is devoted to the time parameter in the never-ending battle to bring profits under control. What we learn when we look at snapshots of the profit-by-product calculation over time is that considerable variation occurs. Market conditions drive changes in selling prices, and manufacturing performance is never static; seasons change and raw material prices fluctuate. The point is that the more knowledge you have about where you are right now, the better control you will have over the ability to generate profit.

Consider the case of semiconductor products in Chapter 6. The selling price of a new product was at its peak at the beginning of its life cycle and quickly began the decay as market demand was met and as third parties began to copy the product. At the same time, costs remained somewhat flat, except for minor improvements across time. If the selling price decay continued, the lines would cross at some point. Obviously, this is the break-even point and that intersection event should mark the termination of that product's life cycle (Exhibit 11.2). You don't want any products in your catalog that cost more to make than you can sell them for. The problem is that you probably don't know, either at all or in a timely fashion, when you cross that line, or perhaps if you even started there. Too many times, I have done an analysis of profit by products and discovered that several popular products have been bad business. The last thing you want is for some products to be eroding your hard-earned profits.

There are numerous ways to take charge of the bottom line and manage this important contribution. What if you dis-

**Exhibit 11.2**   Marking the Break-even Point

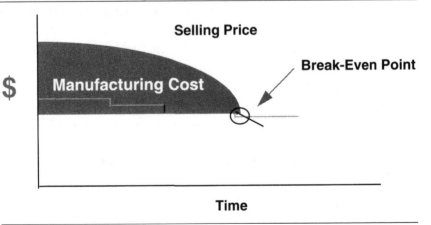

cover that a product line is not as profitable as you desire? What options do you have? Remember that profit has two key elements: revenue and cost.

The logical first step is to consider ways to enhance revenue. Have you considered new markets, new market uses, or markets not influenced by the price precedent currently pinching you? Perhaps you could try price negotiation with your current slate of customers, using detailed cost data that ABM can provide. Customers do recognize that your business is not a charity. I would hope that your attempt at seeking relief via price negotiation would signal, at least, the silent threat that you might withdraw from manufacturing any product you didn't make a profit on (unless contractual obligations must be met).

Perhaps a slight modification to the product would enable you to hold significant value to the line and/or improve the production rates to a level increasing the production efficiency, thus lowering costs. Many discoveries are overlooked when there is no driving force to stimulate our creative juices. One of the greatest assets we have in the United States is our ability to become inspired by a driving force, such as wars, embargos, or environmental threats. We seem to become inventive at an inspired, motivated level when pressure is applied.

Profit should inspire that same degree of inventiveness, driving us to find opportunities for reductions in manufacturing cost. Look for ways to reduce waste, run at optimum rates, improve conversion efficiency, and minimize labor contribution. There is always a way to do something better. I like to take the process flow, diagram it, and label each component with the dollars each consumes along the way. Such a picture points out where to focus your efforts. (*Hint:* pick the big dollar items first.)

Clearly, the last option to consider in this recovery plan is *product elimination*. After all, if you cut some volume out of your production, you still must amortize the cost of all assets over the remaining volume; thus, all other product costs will go up. So, you must find new volume or new products to consume that capacity. Now tell me, why is that so bad? Life follows that same process. We need to accept that some products reach the end of their life cycle. We also need to know when, why, and what we are going to do about it.

I always teach: plan and react, plan and react, plan and react, then allow a product to die as the last resort. But even then, provide a replacement to pick up its place. A "last call" is a big step and should never be taken lightly.

How can you use ABM to achieve profitability forecasting? After all, ABM is a measurement tool that looks at current performance. What mechanisms can be employed to use this information as a forecasting tool? Doesn't ABM just measure one side of the profit calculation (cost)? The answer is yes, of course, but many of the controllable cost factors are captured in this measurement. But a time-history showing the behavior of individual components of cost and their relationship to changes in production rate and other degrees of freedom begins to characterize the profit contribution behavior of your enterprise. These individual behaviors can be modeled in a classic way, allowing you to use good judgment in predicting how each element of cost might behave when you look beyond the margins of historical performance. What you discover in real life is that most historical behavior covers a broad enough range that, at some point in time, you already have history at the extremes for each individual activity and a significant stretch may already have documented behavior data points. So, you can say that this is a behavior that has been achieved before, so you should be able to do it again.

Some think of forecasts merely in terms of what business they can gather in their market at some point in the future. Certainly that is a component of the forecast, but if revenue and cost must be considered, then I have to find ways to predict both, if I'm going to forecast profit. I've already laid the groundwork for the variability in cost. Don't forget to include that factor in your forecasting. Time is one of those variables that we seldom include in our forecasting efforts.

Clearly, profit contribution forecasting can be valuable in planning production, setting optimal rates, and considering the business case for producing at optimum and building a little inventory or shifting mix to maximize profit. Perhaps learning how to reduce the penalties for bumping into constraints might be an outcome of improved knowledge about where improvements are needed (and what they are worth).

Certainly, life-cycle analysis (that is, tracking over time and understanding the performance of a product that has external pressures on price) is enabled by a tool such as ABM. With the ability to take frequent snapshots of existing product costs, you can generate management actions appropriate for those products and set up knowledge-based decisions for new products as well. I can easily see product line managers being held accountable for profit contribution and ABM being the tool for supplying that measurement.

All of these efforts and points of focus seem aimed at understanding and managing the business in such a way that good business is pursued and bad business is understood and identified and measurements are in place to help you manage your way out of a predicament. Knowing the contribution to profit of every product is essential to being in control of the bottom line.

## CHAPTER 11 HIGHLIGHTS:

A. Volume versus profit.

B. Ranking by business parameters.

C. Empowerment.

D. Plan for profit.

E. Life cycle.

F. Improvement/recovery opportunities.

G. Forecasting.

# CHAPTER 12

# Architecture of a Real-Time Cost System

I learned a great deal about the fundamentals of design from an architect. He wanted to know about our family's lifestyle so he could understand how we would use the dwelling he was being asked to design. He wanted to know the importance of each functional area and something about our values so he could stay focused on the things we believed were important.

The concepts of real-time cost management must be applied in much the same way as the architect's skills. This information has to have value for the user or it will simply be set aside. Knowledge of where the value lies is key! It also helps to define the sources and origins of each component of the cost pyramid. Every cost structure is different: some have 80% of the cost in raw materials; others have only 10% to 15%. It is imperative to begin one of these evaluations with a clear understanding of how you intend to use this knowledge and how focused you are (that is, what your values are) for each of the categories of cost. In that way, you will know how much detail you need in order to satisfy the level of analysis necessary for this result to be beneficial. Problem analysis becomes a key design criterion for real-time profit management.

The basic requirements for an activity-based cost system (ABC) include the ability to get information from resources such as:

1. General Ledger
2. Purchasing
3. Process Production Control
4. Inventory Management
5. Maintenance Work Orders
6. Shipping and Receiving
7. Payroll/Labor Accounting
8. Planning/Production Schedule
9. Order Entry/Sales
10. Decision Support System (EIS)
11. Laboratory/Quality (LIMS)

Although each of the listed items is functionally a unique source, in reality each may represent numerous physical interfaces. For example, you may have 5, 10, or more production lines, each with its own production control and production measurement system.

The fundamental information required for ABC comes from unit costs and measurements of consumption. The design of each product cost model must incorporate access to both for every element of the list of activities consumed by that product. Since many of the activities are shared, some measurement methods must be devised to determine an equitable way to assign each activity to its consumed share.

This design and layout of the raw source data becomes a key parameter in the efficient and successful design of ABC models. It is important to keep data synchronized in the same groupings and by sample time. This is crucial to the validity of any results driven by this type of decision support system. I prefer to construct the cost models with a software tool that encourages some structure (for example, *Easy ABC* by ABC Technologies, Portland, Oregon), but it is feasible to build them in a spreadsheet tool. The raw data are much more manageable when used with a database of some integrity. You will find that the combination of tools that you select can make or break your effort. Some interfaces (Easy *ABC* to Oracle, for example) already exist and greatly reduce the efforts necessary to access data and to return results.

Do not underestimate the effort needed to understand the content and makeup of accounts in the General Ledger. Understanding the content of GL accounts and how each is consumed by your activity will require an intermediate step to break the number down so that you can measure its consumption. Look for the origin of each accumulation of spending; it will be made up of some unit cost and some measurement that represents the volume consumed.

The basic architecture of the activity-based model appears in Exhibit 12.1. The raw data are captured, along with the time stamp of their sample time, and deposited into the relational database. Special interfaces will need to be constructed to provide this communication lineage. The cycle time will need to be determined through analysis of the dynamics of each data point. Remember, you will be gathering both basic unit or total cost information and measurements that reflect usage or consumption of each cost element.

This raw data become the input to the activity-based cost models. Interfaces between most relational databases and *Easy ABC* already exist. (Your choice might take interfaces into consideration.) The cost models then calculate each

## Figure 12.1   Activity-Based Model Architecture

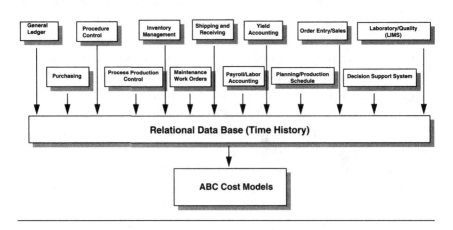

activity cost and assemble the modules of cost, according to the parameters chosen for each product cost model. Both the modular activity costs and the larger model costs for each product are then returned to the database to be stored with

## Figure 12.2

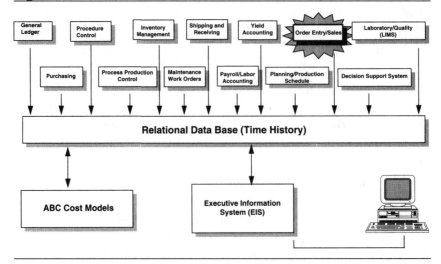

the time-segmented raw data, completing the database record for each time-slice.

At this point, you have created very important information, but no one has had an opportunity to use it. I've mentioned that profit is a valued resultant that uses cost. Some form of reporting must be constructed to formulate the kinds of information presentation and inquiry support that satisfy your business needs. Obviously, use of order or sales data with ABC cost results will support a level of profitability analysis not previously available (Exhibit 12.2).

The time-history is of particular value in diagnosing when and why variances occur. The ability to reach down to activity levels should be supported by your executive information system (EIS) (see Chapter 9 for more detail), which permits examination, determination, measurement, and historical tracking of improvements (and Hawthorne-effect decay) of individual activities within your processes (Exhibit 12.3). Product managers and production process owners should

**Figure 12.3**   A Time-History of Performance

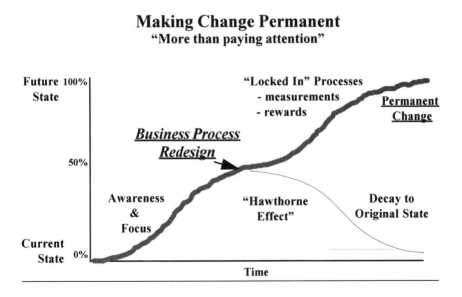

have particular interest in (and/or responsibility for) the cost performance histories of each activity and its parts, as well as the cost of the product itself. How else will they be able to know where the opportunities for product cost reduction really lie?

## CHAPTER 12 HIGHLIGHTS:

    A. Ways to deliver value.

    B. List of basic information sources.

    C. Time-stamping and synchronization.

    D. Architecture-costs.

    E. Architecture-profit and EIS.

    F. Opportunities for cost reduction.

# CHAPTER 13

# Implementing a Real-Time System

An on-line, real-time ABC measurement capability enables you to successfully measure the elements necessary to calculate profitability. The issues of compatibility and time synchronization of measured costs with specific orders are not trivial, but they can be surmounted with today's computing capabilities (bar-coding, for example). The secret of success comes from the ability to collect the preponderance of the costs. It is one thing to have knowledge of how much individual elements actually cost (in terms of cost per pound or per unit of value); it is yet another to know, precisely, how much is being consumed by the manufacturing process.

The key, therefore, is the ability to measure the actual consumption of raw materials, energy, manufacturing cycle time, support activities, and associated logistics costs in order to compile a realistic picture of how costs are being consumed. If you think of your business as a giant system that consumes dollars and produces product, you will be getting the right frame of reference for how this profit measurement system is going to work.

We will examine the priorities, the methods of measurement, and use of cost driver information.

In most cases, raw materials represent a majority of the cost of the finished product. Thus, we place the highest priority on the precise measurement of these materials. It is extremely important to recognize some basic principles of good business in the acquisition and consumption of raw materials:

1. Pay only for what you receive.

2. Minimize your handling losses (spills).

3. Avoid off-speculation production.

When materials are received, measure the quantity sent against the order. Never take sellers' or shippers' word for how much they deliver. I guarantee that your innocence will be short-lived. Know what you have and how much you paid for it. The biggest gap in costing products today is the "tank running dry" before you have consumed what you thought you bought.

(I believe in "paying on consumption" as a philosophy of materials purchasing, but that's a subject for another book.)

Today's instrumentation/material delivery systems provide a good source of input for the cost driver of raw material consumption. If you can access your production control system, there are several pieces of information that will be important for you to capture for use:

1. Consumption of each raw material stream

2. Yield (production) of product

3. Production rate (to be used later)

4. Energy consumption

Clearly, the amount of raw materials consumed times their unit cost is the basis of the costing equation. Knowing the yield then permits the dollar per unit of product to form the basis for product costing, not final production multiplied by some standard product formula.

Another significant expense is the amortization of the facility. Knowledge of how much time each product consumes of that facility seems a fair basis for this calculation. Therefore, production rate can be used to effectively provide a prorated share of facility cost.

Energy costs can be measured directly, giving another direct measurement of expense; when coupled with production rate, they provide a sound basis for another of the elements of cost.

One quickly begins to notice that the 15 to 20 major activities that contribute to the cost of a business can all be accounted for in some way or another, but not all are dynamic in nature. Some vary with recipe, some with quality, some with production efficiency, but some have no direct relationship to the actual manufacturing cycle.

For example:

1. It costs about the same to capture and enter a large sales order as a small one.

2. You never know when some item will break and require maintenance.

3. Shipping costs are probably out of your control and may vary through the year.

Yet, these remain very real costs that must be borne by the product. Their capture must be just as significant in the accuracy of their measure and in the recognition of how each product consumed its expense. The more frequently you capture these types of expenses, the less troublesome is the method of matching cost to product.

*But note:* The dynamics are going to be very different, but it is all right to mix sample-time frequencies. When you maintain a common frame of cost (unit of production), the results can still be accumulated.

Your sample times should be the result of some significant amount of study of the degree and rate of variability of each cost driver. You want to sample frequently enough so that you don't miss excursions.

Only analysis of data, plotted as a time history, will permit you to select appropriate sample frequencies.

It is also sometimes necessary to provide a reconciliation method for correcting for improper assumptions or inventory losses/spills. For example, you will have to make an assumption about annual production capacity in order to appropriately use production rate for a time period as a loss for assigning facility amortization expense. After you have been collecting data for a while, you can begin to use running average numbers.

A sudden excursion can create a sudden impact unless some form of averaging is employed to allow a gradual correction of the appropriate magnitude. I prefer to use the filtered approach because of the lessened psychological impact of a sudden change in cost when no significant change in operations has occurred.

The summation of all costs within the ABC model must be synchronized with the actual selling price of the product. I have used bar coding for matching inventory to sales price and I have used production schedules for large custom orders to coordinate the right cost with the right selling price.

Your manufacturing operation is probably not aware of the fact that different customers cut different deals to pay different prices for the same product. What's more, your sales organization and your shipping department often add extra, unplanned expenses by agreeing to special packaging, last minute changes to the order, special expediting, and unique but inefficient methods of loading and shipping. A good costing system will measure the activities generated by all of these types of add-ons and cost them appropriately—then tack those costs onto that particular order. It is quite amazing to see the add-on costs that some customers never have to pay.

When the "real" cost is charged against the actual selling price, the profit margin for that order becomes apparent. Records set up by customer and by product then begin to compile the basic performance history that is so vital to the strategic planning of the business.

The tactical values are noted by the ability to see the frequent updates in those individual activities (and to see their net impact on the cost of product). The real-time nature of frequent updates is enormously diagnostic in the control of costs.

I believe strongly in keeping time-histories of these frequent measurements. The trends you can see allow you to anticipate and circumvent variances from target. They also allow later study and diagnosis of ways to improve the manufacturing processes (based on cost of operation).

The ability to see a day, a shift, or a few hours of financial performance and to identify the various elements of the cost equation can be of immense value to the manufacturing operation. Chapter 15 is dedicated to the subject of how to harvest the value from this information, but suffice it to say that tomorrow's manufacturers will have to be intimately aware of their costs, as well as their productivity, to be competitive.

## CHAPTER 13 HIGHLIGHTS:

A. "Big cost" drivers measured first.

B. Raw material measures for process controls.

C. Need to measure raw materials.

D. Consumption measured, not standards.

E. Elements of cost that are real-time candidates.

F. Unpredictability of some costs.

G. Variation in sample-time frequencies.

H. Need for cost and selling price synchronization.

I. Add-ons—potential profit disasters.

J. Time-history: a trend of costs by activity.

# CHAPTER 14

# The Elements of the Cost Equation

It is important to know just exactly what is included in this magical equation that is supposed to help manage the bottom line. Taking the step from the classical baseline of studying dollars already spent to this new technique of measuring how and where those dollars are spent deserves considerable study and understanding.

First, let's determine what the conventional cost-accounting elements are and then look at how an ABC model is constructed. I want you to see that the assembly of ABC elements is (and should be) very different from the traditional construction of costs.

Conventional cost accounting is constructed by summing all the spending from several departmental accounts that have been designated as being part of the *direct* cost of goods and adding it to the *indirect* expenses accumulated from the General Ledger. One example is the cost associated with (or charged to the account of) the operation of the production line. Now, surely you will recognize that these standard costs may or may not include *all* the actual labor costs and *all* the carrying costs for the assets employed, if some problem came up and extraordinary efforts were required to complete that order.

These costs are derived from accounts that emanate from the traditional budgeting process. They have been categorized by departmental boundaries and have little or no breakdown by process function. That is, they are descriptive of a departmental spending plan, but not of what was actually spent for each production cycle. Remember it is our thesis that we can manage better if we know the profit margins of each production run. A data source of spending by department or by some organizational entity is not well enough defined to instruct us about the profit margin of a particular product.

I have observed many times that a few products that consistently require extra effort to produce, consume the major share of the support organization's efforts. So, I have to ask myself if all the products should equally share the cost of that support service. I don't think so! I believe that the production object that consumes a resource should have to bear the cost of that resource and justify the bottom line cost in some legitimate business case.

Now, the traditional cost accounting methods summarize all these departmental spendings and use some form of allocation to distribute those costs across the total production. Typically, that allocation method is volume based. I have previously castigated volume-based allocation methods as inappropriate for accurately portraying how an object consumes cost during the manufacturing cycle. Nevertheless, after these costs are summed (and remember the time frame of this type of data collection), some mechanism is applied to try to make sense of the profit or loss picture for production. I would never dispute that the gross, or overall, measurement didn't tell the compelling story of whether or not the company was sound, but I contend that another level of profit management can be attained with an improved method of measuring the cost of each individual product made within this common manufacturing facility.

Now, what makes the ABC model a better way to measure these costs? To begin with, ABC models are premised on a process perspective of the business. In other words, one looks at the events required to manufacture the product, at the resources required to support manufacture of it, and at the consumables required to build it. Support activities must also be considered, such as shipping, sales, invoicing, advertising, and a seemingly endless list of other activities. By looking at the business as a collection of process activities and measuring the consumption of each and every activity, in a resolution fine enough to correlate that increment of measurement to the specific product being produced at that moment, you can begin to see how ABC methods will allow the assembly of all of these components of cost in much the same way as a favorite food is created from a recipe. Each product will have its own recipe or cost model that accumulates the costs of those resources that are consumed during its manufacture.

This all seems like a ridiculously complex way to answer a question as simple as "How much does it cost?," but the truth is that we rarely understand the answer. ABC cost models are detailed and contain many elements of unit cost and cost drivers for a myriad of cost elements. It is not difficult to use a little imagination and compose the form of the model such that they are actually self-documenting. Besides, if you think this is complex, ask your CFO to explain the rationale behind the choice of the chart of accounts in the General Ledger.

Our existing cost accounting systems were developed because we needed some way to guide our management towards good business decisions. The financial database was the only source of information that was readily available. It was never designed to give the detailed information that ABC can provide.

Let's take a look at some of the activities that are typically modeled for inclusion in an ABC equation:

1. One of the most obvious ones is the measurement of each element of raw materials. Many times this segment of cost represents a majority of the overall cost of a product. Remember that the measurement must reconcile with inventories and purchases and some complexities must be built in to the raw consumption measurement system to truly compensate for losses and shrinkage. It is not enough to know how much material is being consumed; you must also know the unit cost of each particular lot of material being consumed. Many contingencies are defined here. It is necessary to be able to track material by lot in order to capture this level of finite cost measurement, and it can be done.

2. Production cost is not always a line item in the conventional cost accounting system, but I believe it is one of the most misunderstood and misapplied costs in the industry. I related a story about this expense in Chapter 1. My contention was and is that certain products and certain production schedules call for and consume production facilities in vastly different quantities. The same exact product may be produced at different rates and at different times, and thus it consumes different amounts of the available production capacity. Remember, my thesis is that each unit of production should be charged with the resources it actually consumes. (Now do you see why a product has a dynamic fluctuation to its cost behavior?)

3. Maintenance is one of those categories that is often a high-cost activity but is indirectly related to the actual

product. Yet, some of those difficult-to-make products definitely require more maintenance than others. It is up to the model development team to identify if there are any products that should bear a more appropriate portion of this equipment- or facility-related expense.

This list should go on to detail about 12 to 20 major activities that cover all the categories of cost in a company. Items such as "indirect overhead" may end up being the catchall for the loose ends, but all of the cost items must be contained in this ultimate collection system.

Many sources of information must necessarily be interfaced. You must be able to access data from the following systems or departments: General Ledger, purchasing, scheduling, production control and measurement, shipping, time accounting, and utility consumption. Others will crop up as essential elements as well, so be prepared to utilize the vast and imaginative resources of your computer support organization as you design this system to automatically capture each and every piece of information necessary to provide these ABC models with accurate and timely data.

## CHAPTER 14 HIGHLIGHTS:

A. Conventional cost accounting versus ABC.

B. Measurement periods—short or long.

C. Costs for indirect expenses.

D. Standard costs versus measured.

E. Actual or forecasted.

F. Raw material measurements.

G. Production line expense.

H. Maintenance costs.

# CHAPTER 15

# Harvesting the Value from ABC

Today's manufacturing companies have cost structures that are difficult to understand or measure. Those that manufacture multiple products in the same plant and sell those products to a large number of clients have the opportunity to gain both strategic and tactical value from the application of activity-based costing (see Chapters 7 and 8 for a discussion of strategic and tactical benefits).

In evaluating opportunities for improvement, I often find that a client's sales distribution offers numerous clues about where to look for potential benefits. I often discover that a high percentage of that company's customers and, conversely, a tiny percentage of its revenue reside with a large number of clients. The absolute numbers of this basic measurement often direct me to investigate whether my client has an understanding (and a true measurement system) of just how much it costs to deliver a large or small order.

The cold hard facts often reveal that most of the profits are generated by a few choice contracts, while many small orders erode those profits.

Remember: *You can't manage profit if you can't measure cost.*

I usually ask if my customer can tell me about profit margins by quarter or by year, by order size or by location of manufacture. I want my clients to know profitability by product, by order (and thus, by customer), and by territory (or salesperson).

With this type of knowledge, the executive could hold the process owner accountable for the performance of a manufacturing or business process (Michael Hammer's book on *Reengineering Business Processes* is important here). Or this knowledge could also provide fact-based decision support for strategic leadership in what products to promote (those that generate profit) and how to measure and track continuous improvements. Certainly, manufacturing personnel would need a gauge that tells them how well they run their process—in terms the owner appreciates. Even the planners and schedulers will discover that historical cost behavior can be used to forecast the profitability of a scheduled mix of products—before they actually enter production. Now that's revolutionary!

We do know that knowledge of the cost of your major business processes is an eye-opening piece of information. *And* when a measurement system is put in place to keep that information visible, improved behavior begins to be noticed.

You must start your quest for improved financial performance by clearly understanding a basic principle: the reason we are all in business is to make a profit.

By now, you should have a grasp of the principles of activity-based costing and of how cost information can be used in a larger scheme of integration with General Ledger data, sales and process control data, and others, to present a reporting system of product and customer profitability. You should also remember that "profit measurement" is a tool for driving the behavior of an organization in the direction of improved performance and is not a direct replacement for any of the financial reporting systems. The key is that timely availability of profit performance at many different levels—product, activity, task—provides an opportunity to respond with appropriate behaviors.

The very structure of ABC permits the capture of the cost of every activity, task, or subtask that occurs in the manufacture of a product. This precise measurement process can provide quick facts for decision support, in contrast to the "after-the-fact" reporting capability of conventional cost accounting systems (Exhibit 15.1).

We begin to understand the concept of "value" by learning how and where products consume cost. Many lecture and reading hours have been consumed in the past decade learning about "value-added" (such as adding catalyst to provoke a reaction), or "non–value-added" (NVA) activities (such as movement of incompleted products to a storage area while waiting for components or more raw material). The fact remains that many NVA activities are still essential steps in the manufacturing configuration. I am suggesting that there is value in understanding the variability in just how those

**Exhibit 15.1**   Timely Information for Remedial Action

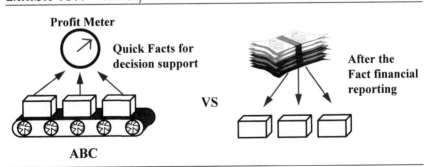

**Exhibit 15.2**  Determining Minimum Run Size

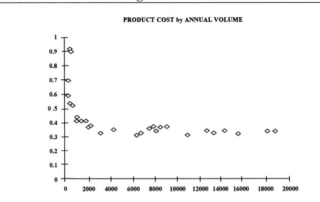

activities behave over time. By time-stamping data and creating a time-history of how activities' costs behave, we learn that cost is dynamic—that is, it has a life of its own. In fact, some days are better than others; some production runs behave differently from one run to the next; and you will discover that run size is a significant variable in the cost equation (Exhibit 15.2).

A time-history of the details of each task, of each activity in the ABC equation, can warn of (or diagnose) important and expensive trends toward nonprofitable performance, allowing notification and corrective action before those profits erode or slip away. I like to use statistical process control (SPC) charts (Chapter 17 provides more detail about SPC use in real-time costing), to see activity cost trends and to alert me to cost excursions before they destroy my ability to meet profit goals.

Implementation of this concept of accessibility to current and actual business performance is a distinct competitive advantage. The ability to understand the variability of profit by product mix, order size, special handling requests, production rates, and so on enables management and operations to strategically manage the bottom line (Exhibit 15.3).

## Exhibit 15.3

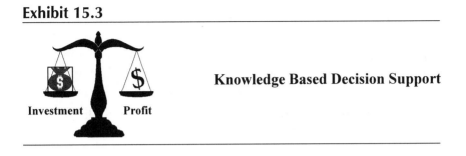

**Knowledge Based Decision Support**

Once you see how activities represent dollars, you will be able to recognize when each activity is under control (and when it is *not*). Measured costs, in the area of manufacturing activities, especially, should be treated as a process control variable. Some attention to their performance can yield valuable information about how costs are controlled. This is primarily applicable to those cost activities whose cost drivers are measured in real time (e.g., consumables measured within the process control system). Variations should be expected. I never expect a flow rate to be 100 percent stable, so why should I expect the consumed cost (of that flow or one that includes that raw material) to be absolutely constant. ABC, implemented in a frequent cycle of updates, will show these variations as costs that bounce around. Now, you can always run a long lag time averaging function to smooth these out, but the fact is that cost consumption is just as dynamic a variable as any of the consumables in the process.

The point to note is that nobody has *ever* seen variable costs vary. That behavior will scare away the strongest supporter of profit measurement. The fact is that we have been conditioned, as a culture, to expect rigid, stable, fixed values for cost. Even though we may understand and do our best to educate those who will have access to the data, you should expect a knee-jerk reaction when they first see how the cost of an activity moves around in real time.

There is great value in the diagnosis of this dynamic behavior. Consider the first few moments of a transition from one product to another. The first production is usually at a slower rate and is off spec, achieving profitability later, after stabilizing the quality and speeding up the production. The profit contribution, plotted throughout this startup period, tells us some very interesting information (Exhibit 15.4).

For example, early in the production, before the product is on spec, the rework penalty (or lower scrap value) means that these first production pounds are being produced with no chance for profit, so the negative contribution to margin must be offset by profit made from good product made later. Most quality deficiencies are quickly corrected, but that negative accumulation must be offset by an equal amount of positive contribution, bringing us eventually to a break-even point. Have you ever determined how to *measure* minimum order size? This form of profit measurement and accumulation is one way to measure the minimum size order (break-even volume and a minimum acceptable profit margin). Now, this is not so significant when production runs are huge and involve little transition. But remember what I said about looking at clues about how your products are sold. How many small orders do you squeeze into your production schedule?

**Exhibit 15.4**    Profit Performance Curve (as a Function of Time)

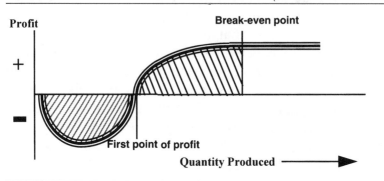

Do you have a minimum order size (or do you know the cost penalty for a small order)? I also find few customers who can tell me what it costs them, in terms of dollars or in terms of capacity, to reprocess the off-spec material that they rework to bring back up to specification.

A hierarchy of values is available when pertinent and appropriate measurements of business performance are implemented (Exhibit 15.5). The most basic one reminds me of the behavior I always observed when I began to speak about discipline to my children: behavior improves when one acquires knowledge that he or she is being observed. You don't even have to do anything—just discuss your objective and your planned method of observation and an immediate (although temporary) improvement will occur.

The next tier of improvement comes with the actual implementation of the measurement: deliberate modifications of individual activity management occur when direct feedback of performance is available. Further, knowledge of current performance levels supports the theme of continuous improvement agendas.

**Exhibit 15.5**  Life Cycle Pyramid

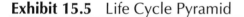

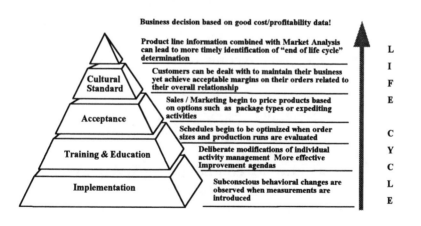

Next, schedules begin to be optimized when both minimum order sizes and the relationship and behavior of cost/volume are understood. Sales and marketing will begin to get in on the act, studying price sensitivity and variabilities that result from certain special handling activities.

Partnering with suppliers and customers also becomes a possibility when you gain confidence in knowing when you can make concessions and still maintain your competitive advantage. The full impact of how to harvest value from this new, timely piece of information will not be understood until it's in your hand, tracking performance and product life cycle and managing profit proactively.

There are always a number of surprises that come as you attempt to enhance your organization's performance with these new pieces of information (or perhaps, your experience is that your organization just doesn't respond well to any kind of new information). After all, cost information has been given out sparingly up to now. What has been available were quarterly or annual averages, with little or no information about the selling price (or "deals" with customers) so one could deduce the profit.

So, little visibility occurs and almost *no* dynamics are understood by the manufacturing group. Therefore, we must fill this void with some education about what this information is, how it is derived, and what action we expect from it. Expect a learning curve; you are going to experience one.

ABC results are painfully accurate. It's always a shock to discover that our company is not functioning as well as we thought. We generally respond to that kind of news with denial. We also react negatively to the recognition of how variable cost activities really are.

It is imperative to condition organizations to expect dynamic movement in the calculated costs of individual activities. They should be taught to expect variation and to recognize cause and effect. The most important linkage is between their actions and the response to the cost calculation. Preparation of the operating group—from consideration of what to expect *and* what actions will be allowed in response—should be the first step.

Some companies are using ABC measures as the basis for incentive programs. Recognize ABC for what it is—one piece of an improved knowledge-based decision support system.

## CHAPTER 15 HIGHLIGHTS:

    A.  Sales distribution offers clues.

    B.  Profit by product and by customer.

    C.  Knowledge of cost behaviors.

    D.  Timing of availability of costs.

    E.  Detailed timing enables better planning.

    F.  Competitive advantages.

    G.  Cost variabilities.

    H.  Minimum production size.

    I.  Decision support value pyramid.

    J.  Integrating cost into your culture.

# CHAPTER 16

# The Minefield of Real-Time Information

When data are collected from actual measurements, the results will be the *factual* representation of that action's behavior. What might that behavior look like? It will have the same dynamic frequency as the real-life data, but few people, if any, are accustomed to seeing measurements change with a frequency that is a real representation of life. In fact, the predictable behavior is that people will deny that the data should have any movement at all and will react as though they are walking through a minefield.

Data validity becomes the first issue to confront the process owner when the source is real time. It is extremely important to have the acceptance by the users of the validity of the data. When variability becomes an issue, it is too late to plan a course of credibility recovery. The issue should never have arisen in the first place. When a specific set of data has a lot of variability, study it. For example, examine the source to

111

see if pump strokes are causing fluctuation or if there is any other identifiable cause of the variation. You should then make a judgment call as to how the data should be presented for use. That is, does the data need filtering (by averaging the last several values)? Does it pass all the credibility tests of being within acceptable value limits and the rate of change test to determine whether a value could ever change so fast? The concept of *data validation* should always be applied, but especially when data are acquired in real time.

What kinds of concerns occur with real-time data? Most data are captured by some electrical means such as a differential pressure cell with a transducer or a thermocouple. These devices are installed out in the process area to provide computer-compatible signals for production control or a process control system. Much can happen to devices that are installed in a manufacturing area. They are exposed to various environmental conditions and are subject to abuse, corrosion and deterioration. Some have been known to fail from the extreme temperatures of the manufacturing area in which they were installed. These circumstances dictate that caution be exercised in using data retrieval directly from field or factory floor locations. So the very life cycle of the sources of real-time data dictate that you make provision to validate the results of their measurements.

Other problems occur with sources of measurement systems. Construction workers cut through them, put torches on them, and apply mechanical leverage to their physical mountings in ways that occasionally destroy them. Wires are cut and broken, and connections work loose or corrode. All these possibilities dictate that reconciliation with ranges of expected results be made in the use of data that come from these types of field devices.

An example might be if a flow measurement suddenly jumped from 250 gpm to 500 gpm in a few seconds. This movement just isn't possible; it violates the test of being within the range of expected results. But how do you detect that event automatically?

More sophisticated validity checking is also recommended. *Material balances* are a way to match all of the components flowing into a process with the volume of materials flowing out. It takes a collection of all the input measurements' sums to be compared with the sum of everything on the output side of the process to complete this validation method.

Sum: Input flows should equal Sum: Output flows.
Tolerance should be close to zero.

When a material balance tolerance number begins to creep away from zero, you know that something is wrong, and the values contributing to that calculation are suspect.

It is extremely important to recognize that all the information used must be taken from the process at the same time. Yesterday's input flows cannot be matched with today's production to test that inputs and outputs balance. The value in a material balance is that you will know that your instruments are all in calibration and that the production is at steady state. You will be able to detect a leak or a spill. You will see when a measurement is askew and is causing the material balance to fail the tolerance test.

Field data will normally be used in a number of different ways. Cost information will utilize the measurements of consumption and will be assigned overhead expense based on factors such as production rates. What are the consequences of erroneous values being used and what precautions can be taken to avoid those erroneous results?

Data validation is a special skill that receives little public attention. Yet, it is one of the most critical of the methodologies employed in data management today. Several techniques may be employed to validate raw information. The first is *magnitude testing:* the comparison of the raw value with the range of expected values.

$$\text{Low Limit} < \text{Raw Value} < \text{Upper Limit}$$

This method of validation captures the occasional data transfer of a value with extra or scrambled digits or the value associated with an electrical short or a broken wire in the measurement circuit. It assures you that the numbers are at least in the range of the expected value.

Another method of validity testing is the *rate of change* test. This method looks at the difference between successive values and compares the differential with an acceptable rate of change. Most values' rate of change can be predicted by either the physical limits of the process or the experience of the person responsible for that part of the operation.

$$\text{Value n minus Value n}-1 = \text{differential.}$$
$$\text{Is differential} > \text{limit?}$$

This method prevents runaway failure of sensor data before the values actually exceed the range of validity. After all, we know that a flow cannot increase faster than the mechanical capabilities of the system being measured.

In the daily use of measured values, I prefer to carry a designation factor—Good/Suspect/Bad—in the record along with the raw data value. This type of designator can be tested by the equation that picks up the data record and should utilize that designator to flag the resultant calculation as Good/Suspect/Bad so that anyone looking at the result would know whether or not the raw data used to calculate this result had validity. This is not an uncommon practice in the field of process control, but it is rarely used with data in strategic costing systems.

Field measurement systems provide us with the ability to recognize events such as recycle streams that allow a percentage of the main flow of product to loop around and reenter the main process again, on a cost-penalty basis, in time to take corrective actions. We need to be cautious, however, in the use of these types of measurements. We must recognize the risk that erroneous measurement values do exist in that environment. Data validation techniques can be employed to minimize that risk.

One of the major problems that arises from the use of results calculated using erroneous field data is in the area of planning. Many strategic plans and decisions are derived from the analysis of financial and cost data. When the raw data were erroneous, seriously flawed plans resulted. Can you imagine a product plan being driven by a conclusion drawn from a peak (or a valley) seen from one data point rather than an average, more representative, performance (see Exhibit 16.1)?

Stranger things have happened. I recall numerous occasions when I simply could not accept the conclusions an LP was giving, even though others did believe them. Those intuitive feelings were my safeguard, although they were very unscientific. I looked for reasons and most often found that the basis data had flaws. The need to make sure that data has

**Exhibit 16.1**  Performance Curve

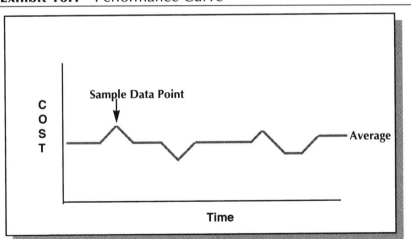

been validated prior to use in any strategic planning or scheduling tool that can impact a business performance cannot be overemphasized.

## CHAPTER 16 HIGHLIGHTS:

A. Dynamic movement of field data.

B. Difficulty accepting variability in cost data.

C. Overcoming variability.

D. Types of field measurements.

E. Kinds of failure in field measurements.

F. Ways to test for validity.

    Individual values.

    Collective values.

# CHAPTER 17

# The Use of SPC in Real-Time Costing

*Statistical process control* (SPC) is an application of statistical data analysis and graphical reporting that can identify trends in data variability not readily noticeable by normal data-tracking methods. Statistical process control has value in the early detection of process movement masked by variability and electrical interference in the recording of the raw measurement.

In the routine capture of sensor-based data and data validation, we employ several sophisticated methods of checks and balances. It was quite some time into the application development cycle of real-time costing that I began to realize that SPC techniques had an application in the portrayal of the calculated values of individual activity cost within the total cost of a product. I was looking for that same early detection capability that SPC provides for raw sensor-based data, when I thought of trying it with calculated activity costs from the time-history of data saved for diagnostic use. I applied the same data capture process that would have been used if the data had been from a flow meter or from a thermocouple (that is, numerous samples taken at frequent intervals, then subjected to grouping and statistical analysis). The result was that X-bar R charts displayed the same real-time trends that measured values would have. This became an extremely effective way to spot deviations from normally expected performance levels.

Let's examine SPC in detail and see how the technique works in its basic form, then capture the essence of how it can be incorporated into the efficient tactical use of real-time cost analysis. (Note: Regular trends will suffice for strategic analysis when the time frame for response is not as likely to cause large cost penalties.)

The basic principle behind statistical process control is to identify the spread of variance from the expected behavior of a measured variable. Observe the data points in Exhibit 17.1. This scatter plot of raw measurements represents a realistic series of calculated costs from an ABC activity that is running in real time.

By taking samples of 5 to 7 data points and using analysis of variance techniques to calculate 1, 2, or 3 sigma deviations, you can then plot the results as a trend and begin to see the movement of variance away from the baseline. This seems like

**Exhibit 17.1**　Scatter Plot of Cost Versus Run Size

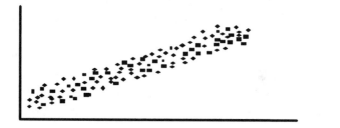

**Exhibit 17.2** Normal Distribution Curve

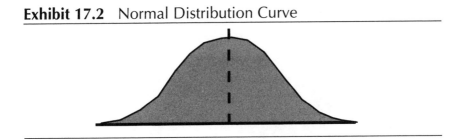

a complex way to observe data, but it is highly effective in seeing behavior before normal methods of trend analysis will show anything. The secret is to understand how variance analysis works. Exhibit 17.2 shows a normal bell curve that we learned was the basis for most data distribution. This shape has a thousand variations and the height and width of the crown of that curve is the key to the type of analysis that I'm describing.

When the top of the curve is wide, the variance has a larger numerical value than when the top is narrow. It is this bell curve shape that we are analyzing when we do the analysis of variance I am referring to as SPC. Thus, when the X-bar R chart trends away from the baseline, the bell curve has changed from a thinner peak of data (Exhibit 17.3) to a wider shaped bell curve that represents data with more variance.

Now, why is this important? Normal methods of data analysis usually include factors such as watching the average performance of a measurement and limits, for example, going beyond a maximum or below a minimum. But normal value analysis does nothing to observe the change of how well a measurement stays on target. What we encounter in real life is that measured variables often begin to fluctuate in their behavior, but their *average* value often remains near the target (Exhibit 17.4). The method of SPC analysis detects this behavior and flags it for you, revealing that this measurement has become erratic even though the average value may not yet

**Exhibit 17.3** Differences in Normal Distribution

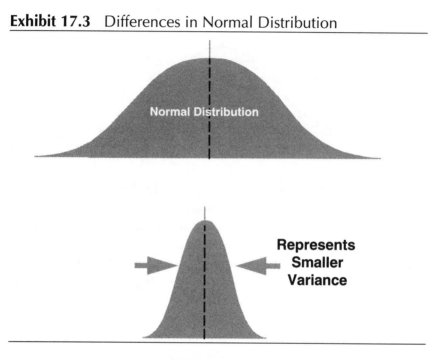

have begun to vary. Variance in a cost value is an indication that something is out of control.

Our whole objective in applying this frequent measurement of cost is to gain control over every element of cost; thus, early detection is a highly desirable behavior of the technique.

**Exhibit 17.4** Tracking Trends in Cost Variation

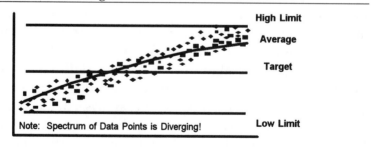

Now, not every variable needs to be analyzed this way. I recommend that activity level summations (probably about 12 to 15 values) be subject to this type of analysis. A number of commercially available software products can provide this capability for you. I do recommend that you engage someone with prior process control experience to advise you in the proper application of this well-tested method. Data sampling is a major key to the success of this method of analysis and is best left to an expert in the field.

My belief is that the value gained is early detection of conditions beginning to go out of control when I can still recover through corrective procedures. I would much rather "spend a little to save a lot" than discover that I've already spent a lot before I even knew it. SPC is a sophisticated method, but one that can be readily applied to real-time cost measurements.

## CHAPTER 17 HIGHLIGHTS:

A. Method to detect "out of control" indicators.

B. Complexity but practicality of SPC.

C. Value of early detection with SPC.

D. Possibility that normal monitoring methods miss important data.

E. Statistical evaluation not required for all values.

# CHAPTER 18

# An Example of ABC Use in Planning

This chapter is written for the refiners of the world. It is specifically written to those in the downstream operation's planning groups who regularly utilize linear programs to maximize the profit available from a barrel of crude. It doesn't take much knowledge about the industry to recognize that some percentage of the barrel has less market value than its cost, while the remainder has positive contributions in varying amounts, offsetting the bottoms that are sold at a loss. The trick is to plan how much heavy material you can afford to convert to achieve that optimum return on investment. Refiners call this the planning function. To see the linkage between the subject of this book and that planning function, it is important to understand how those planning models use representative data to identify maximum profit opportunity.

Each refinery model is constructed to represent the way that a specific refinery separates and converts a barrel of crude into its many finished products. The market price of each of those finished products is closely tracked and carefully analyzed and represents the value each can achieve in the markets served by this particular downstream operation. Now, in and of itself, it is highly important to maintain these product price updates, so that current value is being utilized in the *margin contribution* calculation.

But something is incomplete in this strategic methodology. The margin is the difference between the selling price and the cost to manufacture the product. If so much effort and care are given to maintain and utilize current selling prices, then it would seem safe (and reasonable) to assume that equal efforts are given to keeping costs updated in this complex and highly critical planning tool. But, is cost given the same attention, at the same frequency of update? Clearly, time and again, as I have asked that question, the answer has been "No." In fact, I have seldom been told that cost data were updated more often than annually (*and* the source was almost always that suspect source, the financially based data source).

It doesn't seem unreasonable that operating costs will vary, at least seasonably. Clearly, the ability to separate and convert is a variable that is related to thruput, operating conditions, feed characteristics, and a host of other factors. It seems unquestionably logical that the costs of separation and conversion will be variable as well. The methodology described in this book suggests that the cost of each activity can be measured as accurately as a flow, a pressure, or a temperature. Thus, it would seem that current, measured manufacturing costs could be used in conjunction with current market values to provide that all-important margin calculation with true, representative data.

Historically, I have found significant variability in manufacturing costs. Five to 11 percent ranges of variability are commonly seen in activity-based cost models over time, with short-term excursions being less than seasonal changes. The study of the cost dynamics is also a strong indicator of the degree of control instability and of the response time of the cost variable control aspect of the process. SPC techniques applied to activity-based cost measurements clearly demonstrate when a tight degree of control on cost has been attained.

If a great deal of variability exists in your manufacturing costs and you were to update costs in your planning model as often as you update market values, what might the results be? Two predictable results will follow:

1. *More movement* (changes in recommended operation). One aspect of human nature is resistance to change. But the fact is that the same planning model (with dynamics introduced into its cost elements) will suggest more movement in order to capture larger margin opportunities.

2. *Improved knowledge.* Knowing how often movements should be made and in what magnitude will broaden the understanding of how to gain increased profits from a downstream operation, week to week and season to season.

It is undeniable that the planning model's margin calculation can be made more accurate and more responsive to actual behavior with the employment of cost information from an ABC model. The degree of opportunity is an interesting pursuit. Let's take a cursory look at the potential magnitude of this opportunity:

Assume: 10% fluctuation in operating cost = 10% of
finished value
$30.00 = avg. market value/barrel
(conservative)
500,000 barrels per day thruput

Thus, a simple opportunity calculation might look like this:

$$(.10 \div 2) \times (300,000 \times 365) \times (\$28 \times 0.10) = \$15,330,000$$

| Average variance | Annual thruput | Operating cost per barrel | Value of opportunity |

Did $15.3 million get your attention? It seems to be a huge number. What it reflects is the potential dimension of the blind error in the current way many businesses are calculating the profit margin of their operation downstream.

## CHAPTER 18 HIGHLIGHTS:

A. Industry use of costs in margin calculation.

B. Cost variability.

C. More movement expected from LP.

D. Improved tracking.

E. Size of sample opportunity.

# APPENDIX A

# A Case Study

## I. INTRODUCTION

It began when the CEO called with the complaint, "Why am I experiencing all of these variances to my forecast? We have had the same volume production for three months straight, but a different profit each time."

This manufacturer produced 70 variations on 6 product families. The results of the profitability analysis showed that each product had a different profit margin and a different run-time–to–break-even.

Three of the eight highest volume customers were walking away with the store. They were buying considerably under production cost. This fact was first met with strong disbelief from the top salespeople. Eventually, however, customer agreements were renegotiated.

Since volume goals were the same each week, product mix was not considered in production scheduling. As a result, most small orders were falling below run-time–to–break-even.

The planning horizon was changed from 1 week to 6 weeks as a result.

This example describes the steps of an actual case, re-counting the methods, obstacles, profitability results, and new strategic decisions implemented. You should be able to see the application to your own manufacturing facilities and the possibilities for increased profitability.

## II.  COMPANY BACKGROUND

The client company was a stand-alone segment of a highly integrated corporation. The manufacturing division em-ployed 50 to 60 people; the infrastructure supported several of the businesses. The operation consisted primarily of two manufacturing processes: a basic production process and an enhancing process. Seventy percent of the product from the first process was sold direct. Thirty percent was feed stock to the enhancing process.

Variability in the processes enabled them to create 6 differ-ent product families, and ultimately over 70 different prod-ucts. They were in a commodity business with thin margins.

Customer relationships were based on trust, goodwill, and the long term. The company had been operating in the same manner, under the same agreements, and selling the same products for a long time. It regularly accommodated special requests, including sample runs, irregular quantities, special packaging, and so on. This aspect of the company culture had a dramatic effect on its profit margins.

### A.  Constant Volume, Erratic Profit

Although production was roughly the same each month, prof-its were erratic. Managers found themselves trying to explain why they made $300,000 one month and lost $40,000 the next. It seemed logical that if they produced the same volume, they should realize the same financial performance. But that assumption did not hold true.

They began to look for a solution, a tool that would enable them to measure and control the drivers of profit variance.

In the course of the project, they would see that each product had a different margin behavior; and although the total production was the same, the mix between the different products was causing fluctuation in profit.

## B.   Too Many Variables

It was a complex problem, one the managers could not solve with their existing technology. They could see a number of common manufacturing issues but could not link them specifically to the variance. Intuitively, they could determine some of the problem areas. As experienced people, they could sight specific operational causes and effects. They understood the trade-offs between operating procedures and use of facilities. But there were more variables affecting the profitability picture than they could correlate. Moreover, no mechanism existed to monitor and control what could be identified.

## C.   Losing Profit in the Enhanced Area

The managers suspected that product mix had an effect. Production in the basic process followed normal lines: when volume increased, profit increased. But when production in the enhancing process went up, profits went down.

Originally, the operation consisted of the basic process only. The enhancing process had been added in the belief that the enhanced product would position the company in the marketplace such that these products could command a premium price.

Unfortunately, this was not what happened. Existing customers were accustomed to commodity prices and extensive customer service. They wanted to buy the enhanced product at the same price as the basic one.

As a result, this client was not able to get enough price differential to make the enhanced products seem worthwhile. Should the company even be in the enhanced product business? It needed to justify this secondary business, or discontinue it.

So at the same time that its profit was fluctuating, it was becoming imperative for the company to identify the real cost of the secondary value-added operation.

## D.   Financial Cost Accounting Shortcomings

The client called us saying, "These are probably the causes of the variance. Can you help us build a cost measurement system that will enable us to control the costs in the operation?"

From previous manufacturing experiences, the project team was explicitly able to understand the problem and were confident we would be able to recommend a solution. The only financial tool currently available to the company was the existing cost accounting (derived from financial reports) system. Sophisticated as it was, it could not solve the puzzle. The managers were going to require more resolution of actual consumption of costs.

Traditional cost accounting analyzes spending, not resource consumption. It does not provide the information required to manage profitability. It does not accurately describe where profit is coming from or where it is being lost. In a sense, it describes the financial picture before and after manufacturing, but not during. Yet it is during manufacturing that profit is made or lost. Profit/loss cannot be accurately described or controlled until a system is put in place that actually measures resource consumption, that is, what resources are consumed by which manufacturing activities.

The fluctuation in profit given constant volume confirmed that hidden resources were being consumed. In order to control costs, managers would need an accurate picture of what was taking place during manufacture. Activity-based costing (ABC) was what they needed.

## E.  ABC Deliverables

ABC requires the investigation of every activity in the manufacturing process and of the business processes that support the manufacturing operation. Each step, or activity as it is called in ABC terminology, is completely characterized as to resource consumption, cycle time, raw material cost, and cost of technology. The result is a complete picture of the resources that are consumed and the activities that consume them.

This manufacturing operation lended itself readily to the kind of measurement system that ABC can be. This technique provides the most return for manufacturing sites that produce multiple products and have a sophisticated accounting trail effectively linking sales order prices to customers, to products, to sales personnel, and to sales expenses.

This client met both requirements. It manufactured over 70 products and the accounting computer system was quite sophisticated. Eventually, the ABC model was able to calculate the margin on each product run. Individual runs could be traced back to customers. All runs for a given product could be summed. This provided a complete picture of profitability: profit by product and profit by customer, as well as a definition of the history of variability of profit by size of the production run.

In the ensuing conversations, the ABC project team determined a workable approach. This approach involved how we would gather information from the company's facility as well as what the initial investment of time and effort would be to determine the potential benefits and requirements for the entire project. With the company's agreement, we moved forward. We were able to enter the plant to investigate, so we could relate the actual circumstances to our thought processes and plan a solution.

## F.   Initial Investigation

We began with a walk-through of the facility. Next, our team worked several shifts to observe and document all the activities in the manufacturing process. We gathered information about every activity from receipt of order, order of raw materials, all production phases, customization, quality control, packaging, inventory, and shipping.

This minimum observation allowed us to begin to establish the major manufacturing activities. Many activities needed to be identified and characterized. Each activity consumed a certain amount of resource, for example, energy, raw materials, additives, vessel time, and labor.

Looking further, several support functions needed to be described. These included a sales force that generated business, a marketing group that managed order entry, a financial group that handled credit checks and billings, a purchasing group that procured raw materials, a maintenance group, and a parts warehouse. Each support function had a set of resources, a cost, and a contribution to the overall picture. The result was a description of a surprisingly large infrastructure.

From this initial information, we prepared best case/worst case profitability scenarios. We used data from what seemed to be the most efficient/inefficient processes, plus the most profitable/unprofitable products. As mentioned earlier, the existing financial system enabled us to link specific customer orders with specific sales prices to specific production runs. In each case, we determined the relative margins. This provided a range of profitability.

Using some very cursory modeling techniques, we forecasted what the company's current product mix ought to be generating. What if it were able to do as well as the best case on every product? It would probably never achieve such a goal, but that result became the high end of the scale. Conversely, what if all orders were as bad as the worst case?

From the financials, we could see that the current operation actually achieved only 40 percent of the best case. That figure set a margin of opportunity.

## G.   Executive Commitment

When we presented the best case/worst case scenarios, the executives were shocked that they were operating at only 40 percent of the best case profit potential. It was a somber moment. They turned to make sure the door was closed; they did not want anyone to see the figures. The good news was that there was something they could do to change their current situation and now they had a picture of the opportunity.

Seeing the range of options brought immediate commitment. They wanted to make every effort to bring about improvements. And, of course, if you show an executive additional margin opportunity, he or she will immediately multiply the annual volume by the margin to see the potential gain and will begin to set goals for the improvement team.

Given all the changes that can be made in the scope of a project, the operating mark can be moved up from the bottom closer to the high end to some degree. How many points up from the bottom depends on what the client is willing to do. The determining factor is commitment.

Most executives are measured on their profit performance in some way. Once they see the opportunity, they will do everything possible to capture an improvement option. Given the level of opportunity we provided, the executives of this company made a strong commitment, and the project was off and running. Once the executives were committed to action, we were moving in the right direction. The improvement program had begun, with a measurement system as an integral component.

The foundation of this improvement program was a software measurement system built upon the ABC model. The measurement system calculates the cost of each major manufacturing activity. These costs can then be sorted in numerous ways, including costs by product and costs by customer.

The system is integrated with a strategic planning system that calculates critical strategic information such as the profitability of an order, a client, or a territory. It is a business analysis tool that says "You are making money" or "You are not making money." We call it the *good business/bad business* system. This simple expression seems juvenile, but it is an accurate description. The tactical information combined with strategic profitability analysis and scenario planning forms what we call a *real-time cost management* (RTCM) system.

Immediately, upper-level managers saw the strategic value of this sort of information. It would enable them to focus on deciding what was good business, and what was bad business, at order entry time. It would enable them to trend their sales efforts toward the manufacture of higher profit margin products and could be the basis for a new way to incent sales on contribution to margin.

## III.   THE PROJECT

The task was to devise a measurement that determines what percentage of the manufacturing and support resources is consumed by each product. Most of the time, the client has never analyzed costs that way. The philosophy has been that all activities simply support the business as a whole and are therefore allocated equally across the board, versus being charged to specific products according to resource consumption.

## A. Model Description

The model design was an analytical sequence of events. It was also a discovery process. We looked at the business as though it were a series of processes. There are usually 12 to 15 major events or processes in a business from the collection of orders via a sales organization, or some type of order-capturing process, through the explosion of those orders into raw material requirements, the acquisition of raw materials, the management of raw material inventory, the preparation of raw materials and their introduction into the manufacturing process, down through quality control. There is a direct chain of events. In addition, behind each activity or process are a number of support activities.

We divided the processes into discrete steps and looked at the resources consumed by each step. As many of our other clients have experienced, this client made some startling discoveries. The executives realized that they had $12x$ people in maintenance and $x$ people in sales. It was taking 12 times as many people to keep the operation running as there were people selling the products.

This discovery process alone is invaluable. To quantify in dollars what it is costing to support the people resources, capital investment, asset depreciation, consumables, energy, maintenance, and many other factors, is in itself process changing. When we exploded these items into the many different activities they performed, a lot of overlap was discovered.

Once activities are clearly identified, their value can be determined. We use the terms *value-added* and *non–value-added*. Let's use material movement as an example. An object is picked up here and moved over there. What value did that add? Well, it did not add any. It may be necessary to move it from one place to another because of the physical layout of the manufacturing process, but it does not add any value to the product. Movement consumes resources: people, time, equipment, and space. The question is, then, could the manufacturing area be redesigned to eliminate one or more of these non–value-added steps?

So the operation is broken down into a set of sub-processes, or activities. Each activity is then evaluated for its value contribution. Is it value-added or non–value-added for the amount of resources it consumes, that is, for the total cost of the activity as well as its cycle time? As the non–value-added activities become apparent, the managers can see what can be modified or eliminated. They, in essence, reengineer the operation, cutting out a lot of costs as a natural result of the discovery process.

A model begins to take shape that describes each activity according to its yield, the resources it consumes, and the cycle time it consumes. From these pieces of information, cost can be measured (i.e., the unit cost for that activity can be derived). A model is built for every product or for every sub-component in the manufacturing process. The costs associated with each manufacturing step can now be assembled in modular form using simple algebra.

## B.  Allocation of Shared Expenses

The allocation of expenses that are product specific is straightforward. The allocation of those activities that are not specific to a manufacturing step requires more thought—for example, tax. That is a cost. How do you spread tax across your products? If you use the cost of goods sold, a raw manufacturing cost, as a basis, you have a better foundation than selling price or volume. You could divide the tax by the number of products you have and charge each one the same amount, but that is not right. The allocation ought to be based on something more tangible, more realistic. This technique calculates a proportion of cost for each product. It provides a much more realistic perspective of how to allocate certain expense items. Normal cost accounting systems simply do not provide the information needed to calculate such numbers. Because the ABC model links financial systems with data from the operation, it can provide a more accurate method than traditional models of allocating day-to-day generic costs.

## C.   Characterizing Data

For identifying and dividing costs, we apply the 80/20 rule. If the cost is trivial or insignificant, if it affects only the 13th decimal point, we don't discard it but take a less complex approach to distributing it. On the other hand, if it is a significant cost driver, we attempt to define how that resource is consumed; how it is applied to processes, activities, and products; and what changes it. We identify the functionality of the algorithm that will appropriately apply the cost to the activity that consumes it.

So the basic idea in building the model is to start by thinking of your business as a sequence of processes and to explode each process into its activities. To give you a dimensional flavor of how intricate these models can be, for a $1 billion corporation, there was one ABC model that had 70,000 elements that covered about 100 products. There were 700 cost elements per product.

The number of data points required may seem high, but it takes many pieces of information per product to enable you to measure the costs of each subcomponent of each activity. Given the magnitude of data points, the sourcing and acquisition of data require thorough planning. Several questions must be asked. Where are you going to get a certain piece of information? In what form does it currently reside? Does this data need to be changed into another form in order to be used in the model? How can it be retrieved into the ABC model? What modification of the form of the data, for example, from dollars per ton to cents per pound, is required to be able to use it in the ABC model? Is this measured or calculated? How often does it change and at what rate? How often must it be updated?

Some data are quite dynamic. A good example is the reaction rate in a chemical process. A reaction must be monitored frequently to determine productivity. The reaction rate indicates that the process is yielding $x$ pounds of finished product per minute. It might be a dynamic number. Also, given various operating conditions, the quality of raw material, and the type or life of the catalyst, the reaction may need to be slowed down or sped up. It is critical to accurately describe the rate because yield is an important criterion in the cost factor. It is a variable cost and many other costs are fixed. So the time analysis, the dynamic of each piece of information, has to be examined to determine how frequently it needs to be accessed.

In the same way, the production rate for any manufacturing process will have a high-frequency rate of change. Therefore, you would want to sample it as often as necessary. The model should be designed to make a calculation of manufacturing costs at a reasonable frequency for that element.

Some cost data, such as the depreciation on a piece of equipment, are not going to change. The same number is used every year until the tax accountant changes the depreciation rate. This is a fixed cost that will be assigned to products, based on how much each product uses that piece of equipment.

## D.  Reporting Model Results

It is important to consider the frequency of data collection/calculation and the frequency of the entire model. Data are captured/calculated at a rate that makes sense based on the variability of the data, the natural frequency of change to the data, the importance of the data, and the capabilities of the hardware and software. (Frequency of the entire model can be based on customer request given hardware and software capabilities.)

Some clients are not interested in seeing the results of the model more than once a month. That is not considered real time; it almost goes back to the same frequency as the established cost accounting financial statements. Other clients want to see not all, but certain intermediate pieces of information updated frequently because of this new feedback measurement that has been added to their operations.

The executives in this particular company wanted an accumulation of costs every shift. Because the production runs were set up to produce only eight different products in a month, they did not need information more frequently than per shift. Using shift-to-shift performance indicators, workers were able to answer the question, "Did I do better this shift than last shift?" We actually captured information in the model every few minutes, but we summed it and reported it once every shift.

So the capture of information and the design of the model are determined from the frame of reference of how frequently information does change and how frequently it can be captured and then integrating and presenting that information in such a way that it has value and meaning.

A break-even calculation, for example, is a very high-value piece of information. There is no way financial reporting could provide that piece of information. Frequently measured costs will reflect the increased cost at the beginning of a production run, as changes are being made, and will track the actual costs as it stabilizes, giving an analytical way to measure break-even or minimum order size.

Human judgment is still required.

There are, of course, other more sophisticated factors that eventually could be built into the system. For example, is there a real cost difference between building 60,000 versus 50,000 units of a product? Or do they cost 9 cents each, independent of volume? If 60,000 are made instead of 50,000, can they be made for 8 cents? ABC techniques can help acquire an answer to that question.

The issue of whether your manufacturing assets are effectively utilized was decided at the time of financial reporting, but you still had to make intuitive decisions about your product mix. In the future, with ABC support, you will have this type of information as a basis for making strategic business decisions about expansion business cases.

## E.   Not a New Cost Accounting System

The ABC model captures information from the General Ledger. We have found little resistance to this, except when there has been the misconception that we are building a new cost accounting system. Even though it is very easy to think of the model that way, that is not what it is. This model is not a new cost accounting system. It is a business performance measurement system. The effort is not about a replacement for the cost accounting system, but about improving profit. This client's accounting group got very nervous about all the people getting involved in their business.

The model provides new information to help an executive manage his or her business using cost as the basis for decisions, to manage the business based on profitability, moreover, instantaneous profitability. That is one of the primary goals we are achieving. We are cutting down the time line to accumulate the costs of a product and telling you that the first pound of product that comes off the production line costs you this amount and the last pound costs you a very different amount.

It is not designed to accumulate these numbers and match the financials at the end of the period, although, over the long term, it will. The model is concerned with trends, movements, directions, orders of magnitude, and the factors that drive costs. Once the accountants viewed ABC as an executive decision support tool, they got much more comfortable with it.

## F. Data Gathering

### 1. Manufacturing Processes

Because of the strong support of the business's executives, the operating people accepted the new model, but only to a point. Even in this loyal environment, there was still a certain reservation and lack of commitment. There were questions as to how this change was going to be of value to the people involved in the day by day manufacturing efforts.

**a. Two Profit Centers**  During our data gathering, it became apparent that an effective profitability model would require the two manufacturing processes (primary and enhancing) to be fully separated into different cost centers. About 70 percent of the product from the first process was sold directly and did not involve the second process. Therefore, the volumes through the two plant sections were significantly different. This, then, defined them as two separate operations, that is, two cost centers.

Once we decided to treat them separately, we had to devise a way to split all costs that were previously considered total or whole manufacturing costs. The allocation of fixed costs can be controversial. Do you charge equal amounts of overhead to each process? If not equal, in what portion? Do you charge the products that have had the second process twice the overhead?

Our answer was to look at how much resource each process consumed. We actually measured consumption of each activity in both processes. This gave us a proportion of

cost based on resource consumption. So, there was no allocation argument. This became a fair way of depicting the actual
cost each consumed.

For instance, consider dividing the maintenance costs of
a machine that is used in making several products. The
machine time used by each product is summed over a period
of time. Then total machine consumption is normalized over
that same period. The products that spend more time in the
machine should bear a proportionately larger burden of
maintenance.

Each manufacturing activity had to be analyzed to determine the consumption per process. Was there any difference
in receiving an order for a basic product versus an enhanced
one? We found that there was no additional cost for the second process on the sales side. Therefore, the second process
was not charged again for the sales activity. We analyzed
resource consumption by the two different processes for each
shared activity throughout the manufacturing process and
charged the costs accordingly.

It was hard for the company to make a profit in the
enhancing process. We discovered that this process was the
most troublesome piece of the profitability puzzle. We could
see the company making money in the basic product area,
and then giving it away in the enhancement area. It was strategically important to understand exactly what it was costing the
company to operate this enhancing operation.

Prior to that time, both areas were lumped under one set
of financials. The executives saw only the gross picture. The
process we employed gave them a true cost for the basic product and a true cost for the enhanced product.

**b. Involvement of Workers**   It was our task to create trust
and confidence in the numbers that were being generated as
we built the activity-based costing model and showed that it
really captured true costs. We did that by involving a repre-

sentative from each part of the organization in the model design process. This included identifying the resources consumed, identifying the cost drivers, defining the linkage to the products, and identifying the cost of raw materials and consumables as well as the external resources called on for support.

We went to each resource group within each activity so that we made contact with every element, perhaps not every individual, but every element of the activities that made up the entire process from taking an order to delivery of the finished product. Because we involved them all in the process, no one could refute the resulting numbers. This was not a covert maneuver but part of the methodology that enables us to focus on using client input in the model. The numbers were not an invention of an outsider, but were personally contributed by members of the operation. They could see their contribution as an element of the cost. The numbers became their numbers. From that time forward they could work with the information they provided because they understood the basis of their composition.

By involving people from all aspects of the operation in every step of the cost driver identification process, we accomplished many goals. For one, because they knew that the numbers were not made up by someone else, but a number that they contributed, they developed trust. They knew the numbers' origin; they could explain them, so there was understanding. It also showed them that their activity contributed to the total profitability picture, so there was a self-defined and adopted measure of their own profitability performance. There was ownership and willing accountability. Although the number for each element was only a single cost item, it was something they could see and use. It had some variability. In other words, they could explain it and they could impact it.

As a result of this process, we were able to get a commitment in the early stages from the various parts of the organization that made each contribution to use the data from the model. Once they were part of the process, the commitment came almost automatically. They said, "OK, I can trust that. I know that you are going to use this to calculate overall cost. Can you provide me with some sort of measurement feedback? Can you tell me how much resource I'm consuming? If you can give me some of these measures to help me in my activity, I can make a difference." The measures they were asking for were actually the cost drivers, and it was part of the overall plan to ultimately provide them with that information. This brought about ownership and commitment to use those numbers and to thereby manage their particular activity and individual tasks. For the first time, operations had a "profit meter" to tell them how well they were performing.

## 2. Infrastructure

Although the infrastructure of the ABC model was shared with the other parts of the business, it was not difficult to separate the contribution and cost of this element because of a good paper trail.

The sales unit was involved to achieve information about the selling price of each order. The order entry system was quite sophisticated. Orders were well mapped according to specific levels, products, and customers. Client base and product demand were clear. We could see the activity that was required to support the various mixes of customers and products.

After we analyze the costs according to the products that consume them, we look at costs by customer. There is always at least one customer that consumes more time and effort than any other. This particular client had one customer that would send in 175 small orders each month. In contrast, another customer bought approximately the same volume but sent in only one large order per month. This previously

unnoted imbalance had a great effect on the true cost, and
therefore the profit margin, of doing business with the one
customer versus the other.

# IV.  TACTICAL AND STRATEGIC RESULTS

The vision came to fruition. Now, the company has a model
that links its orders, production schedule, and inventory control; captures data from the General Ledger; and calculates
current costs, so that feedback is based on current information. This system provides a tool to establish the company's
current direction. We called this current measurement *tactical data*.

## A.  Tactical Results

A history of tactical performance allows more important decisions to be made. Now, the executives can answer strategic
questions: Should we stay in this product line with the prices
falling in this commodity market? Should we close out this
product line and look for something to use that displaced
capacity? Should we look for something newer in the marketplace that has less competitive pressures?

It gives executives a mechanism to manage their business
up the scale toward the most profitable scenario instead of
being a victim of circumstance and discovering after the fact
that they are at the low end of the profitability scale. It com-
presses the time cycle of being able to see the impact of smart
business decisions, and it enables them to make those smart
decisions. The final product in this case literally can forecast
profit before the company ever goes into production.

There are still times when a company's *informed* business
decision is to make an unprofitable run anyway. It may be an
unprofitable order size or an unprofitable product at the

request of a client with whom it has a contractual commitment; or it may be making an investment to gain a new client; or it may make the run in order to get a much more profitable product order.

The difference is that now the executives are making decisions based on knowledge. They can quantify the loss before it occurs, and they know the justification behind the loss. They have a knowledge-based decision-making system.

Now they are prepared. They can focus special efforts to contain cost on those product orders that they know are less profitable. They can set a red flag that says to operations, "We have this one coming up that is going to be a real killer for us, so let's get another engineer out here to watch," or "Let's make special efforts to keep our losses down," or "keep our yields up," or "keep the temperature up," or "keep the thruput right," whatever the operating criterion is for that particular product.

## B.   Value Received

What changed dramatically for this company was the knowledge of the cost of production of every product. And in this case study, the finished goods had a tendency to be sold not on cost but on competitive pricing practices. So the value now of having the information of what a particular product run actually cost was highly beneficial from a marketing strategy. The executives knew how much they had invested in that inventory, that specific batch of inventory. When they went to market with that particular batch, they knew exactly what they could negotiate. They knew the break-even level by inventory lot number.

Over the course of the project, we made some interesting discoveries. One discovery was that run size usually had no impact if the order ran over an extended period of days. But runs that took only a few hours had a definite negative impact on profit.

We learned that when they started a new product, there were certain off-spec materials produced that could not be sold. The cost of making these off-spec products, however, was still incurred in manufacturing the on-spec product. Once the product was on-spec, the run had to continue for a certain time before the loss incurred in startup was covered by on-spec profit. If the order size was too small, the break-even point might never be crossed.

## C.  Strategic Results

That information had enormous strategic value because before this effort, it had been a normal activity for operations to make numerous, small-sample runs. They had established relationships with clients who would say, "Make me a small quantity of this for test." And they were just delighted to do that. They had no comprehension of what it cost them to do so. Instead of taking a sample from another large run, they would literally schedule a sample run. No one had ever calculated for them that it was a money-losing size of an order. By plotting the cost of an individual production run, we were able to give them break-even order size, minimum order size, production run information for each of their products, and setup costs for each of their different manufacturing operations. That was *very* beneficial information.

Tactically the managers planned long runs; strategically, they educated their organization to make smarter decisions about trial runs.

They are much smarter now at strategically planning their production runs. In the investigation, we took some specific examples of best case/worst case scenarios of performing all of these extra functions—special volume, special size, unique packaging, certain specified unique handling. All these procedures cost money that is never charged to the customer. The cost has been thrown in as "Well, you are a good customer and I appreciate the order so I'll do all these extra things for you out of good will"; but you had nothing to tell you the cost associated with each of the processes.

Continuing to accommodate such requests erodes profits; but more dangerously, it becomes a norm. Starting at some point in the future, it becomes the new baseline. Then the customer asks for more and you give it. The next thing you know you've boxed yourself into an unprofitable relationship. You rationalize it by saying, "Look at all the things this client buys from us." In reality, this takes you out of good management practice because you simply do not have an appreciation for all the extra factors that consume costs.

The sales force was the first line of resistance we encountered in this company. After we began to develop certain strategic planning information, we saw certain product lines were more profitable than others; in fact, some were outright losers. The executives asked us to convince the various groups to use this information and instruct them on how to get value from it. As we went into the sales organization, we discovered that the salespeople didn't want to hear it. "This customer wants to buy product $x$ and no matter what you say, I'm going to take the order! We've been selling it that way for years! What do you mean you want me to deemphasize that product and to emphasize something else!" They were afraid of losing sales volume.

They didn't see the impact on profit. They were measured on sales volume versus profitability, so this naturally was their perspective. Most sales organizations measure how many dollars of sales the salesperson booked. But in the business world what actually makes the difference between survival and failure is profit, not volume. How much margin did I make? I would much rather sell $100,000 that had a $50,000 margin than $1,000,000 that I lost $10,000 on. It is how much money is left over at the end of the day that is the real measure of profitability. So, we promoted some changes in the measurements. The key was that they were not measured appropriately. They were measured not on profitability of sales, but on volume or dollars. The key is to always look for the dollar profit.

After these efforts, we equipped the salespeople with knowledge that they didn't have before. Now, we could tell them you have this amount of margin on this product and this amount of margin on that product. Previously no one knew the margins. We recommended that they change the sales force performance measurement to profit contribution. "Now, I'm going to measure the sales force on how much profit they contribute. And it doesn't matter if they do it on $100,000 or $1,000,000 sales. I'm going to give them some freedom to negotiate because now we know where the line is, the break-even line." This required the preparation of cost and profit calculations on the sales force's PC's that allowed them to know the margin of a potential order, even as they negotiated.

At the end of the day, volume, of course, plays a role because it magnifies the total number of dollars. The dilemma, however, is that a huge sale with negative contribution to profit is no good no matter what. A company can't make up its losses in volume.

## D.  Costs to Make the Sale

One of the goals that is always a problem for the sales organization is to capture what it really costs to sell a contract. When you get into the expense account records, it is amazing how many times you find that a salesperson has spent as much as he or she generated from a sale in capturing that sale. A salesperson who courts a customer and gets only a $10,000 order may walk away feeling like the victor. But, if someone does a real profit analysis on that order, it may be that the profit was given away before the product was sold.

When the numbers are brought out, a new philosophy begins to develop, which says that the way you manage a business is to know your costs and to have those costs available to you in a format that you can use for making decisions about how you manage your business.

## E.  Customer Sales Profit versus Customer Sales Volume

We presented the first set of results on profitability by customer to a group that included the national account representatives for their larger accounts. This particular company had 8 major customers that bought about 60 percent of their production. Each of those major accounts had a national account representative. Some of those customers purchased *as many as* 16 different products. We began to present profit by customer and showed them the profitability, or lack thereof, of each product line in the volume amounts the customer had purchased over a quarter. The net of quarterly performance was positive, but out of 16 products that one client bought, 12 of them lost money, 4 made big bucks.

When that information was viewed on the screen in graphic form, the national account manager went into denial, "That can't possibly be right, because . . ." and then he hit the nail on the head: "The bonus that I received last quarter for doing business with this client would not have been paid if this were true!" The president of the company replied, "If we had had this information, you might not have received that bonus! If we had known how much stuff you were giving away . . . look at what it could have been!"

To be fair, we do not know if this customer had put the account representative in a difficult situation by saying, "I'll buy some of this, if you'll sell me some of this." In the final analysis, the sales force still has to make long-term relationship decisions. But they are part of an informed business-decision process because they are now making decisions based on profitability of every component of an order for every single product.

They can ask themselves, "Should we even be making this product? If we lose money on it, why do we ship out dollar bills with every pound we sell? We ought not to be making this in the first place. Go ahead and let them buy it from the competition. If we lose money every time we sell it, why should we be selling it?" There may be some sound business reasons why they have to sell it. It may be a by-product that they are making anyway and it just doesn't have a market value. It may be something that the customer says, "I won't buy product $x$, if you don't sell product $y$!" There may be legitimate business reasons to sell a losing low-margin product, but it ought to be a legitimate business decision, an informed business decision, not just a discovery after the fact that they didn't make money on that particular product.

So there was some resistance from the sales personnel because the model presented new information. The very first step after the presentation was to give them access to that information so that they could use it, so they could negotiate better, so they could set prices based on what their costs were. They immediately made this request and made the efforts to learn how to use the information.

## F.   Commitment to Enhanced Business

There were decisions to be made. To begin with, the enhanced product was very costly. The break-even point was beyond the point to which they had been running, and off-spec products made up a considerable percentage of the run. In addition, the way they were handling the marketing or the positioning was inadequate. To make a go of it, they would need to reposition themselves, find new customers, and make a substantial investment in capital equipment. There were definite opportunities out there, but it would take a commitment of time and money to seize them.

Driven by the pressure to justify this business, they looked for new markets for the enhanced product. They became aware of other potential buyers who used the enhanced product as a component for their finished product. Some of these had their own enhancing process as well as another customizing process. Some customers were not willing to purchase the enhanced product at a premium because they still had to do their own customization.

To become suppliers to the other manufacturers would require an additional capital investment so that they could further customize the products before selling them. For them to take on the enhancing and customizing processes was an innovation in the marketplace. So they began to provide customized enhanced products to the other manufacturers. The other manufacturers were pleased to see our client take on a large-scale customizing operation and gladly let their own go.

# V.  CONCLUSIONS

Managers within the client organization had a number of positive reactions to this activity. The following were a few of their comments:

"Once I could actually see the profit contribution of each product, then I could see why we were having such variance. I could also see where the highest margins were!"

"Now we're able to manage profitability at every step from order entry, raw material purchase, delivery [new product and capacity planning, to sales, to production scheduling, to real-time on-line operations decision support]."

"Meeting volume goals does not necessarily mean meeting profit goals."

This project profoundly changed the performance of a business unit. Many changes were made in the way it conducted its business and in the way it incented its employees, with the net result being significant improvement in the bottom line.

# APPENDIX **B**

# Examples of Actual Installations

The following illustrations demonstrate the ways that ABM data have been incorporated in various levels of decision support and planning functions. On many occasions, this same information is used to diagnose operating and economic performance issues.

You will see many examples of profitability and product costing trends. Behaviors shown in trends yield valuable information regarding cause and effect. Various clients have selected various groupings, methods of trending, time segmentation, and presentation methods, but ABM is the genesis of all the basic value derived from these windows into the cost performance of their manufacturing operations.

View this collection of generic examples as ways to capture knowledge from a reservoir of information. This collection crosses a history of many ABM projects and represents prototypical and actual formats of information presentation.

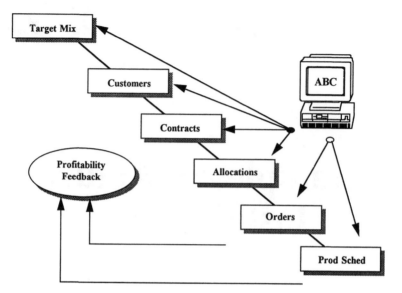

ABM collects information from and influences the way you view the performance of many of the components of the manufacturing processes that contribute to profitability. Feedback as to the impact of each of these driving forces can be seen by clicking on any activity box and having performance graphs pop up that show the relative impact or results from that activity

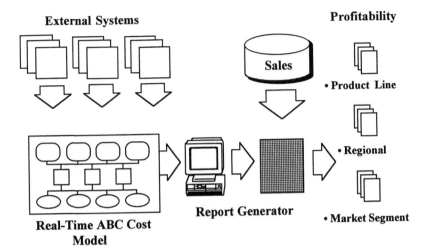

External Systems

Profitability

Sales

• Product Line

• Regional

Report Generator

Real-Time ABC Cost
Model

• Market Segment

It is often beneficial to demonstrate to the casual user how the information flows through the system. Knowledge of the source, how it is collected, and how certain results are obtained is of significant value when presenting results early in an ABC project.

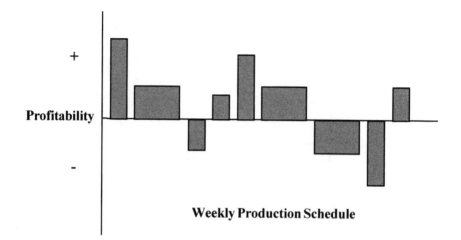

**Weekly Production Schedule**

One of the beneficial applications of knowledge of profit contribution by product or by size of production run is the ability to forecast the contribution to margin of each component of a production schedule. This advance information is par-ticlarly helpful when you begin to incent operations orga-niztions on their contribution to profit. This example demonstrates that not all production runs are profitable. "What if" applications abound in this case.

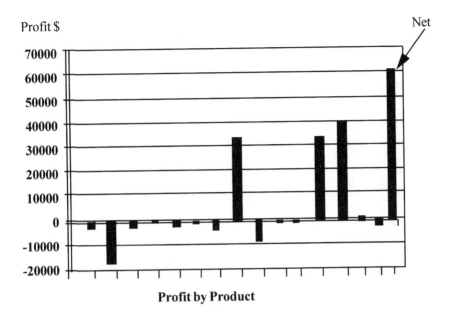

**Profit by Product**

Profitability by product can be cut and reassembled into a use-ful configuration for the purpose of analyzing the profitability of a specific customer. Knowledge of his or her buying pat-terns, specific requirements, and prices negotiated in con-tracts will quickly lead you to promote more of the "good business" and less of the "bad."

## Selected Customer Profit Summary

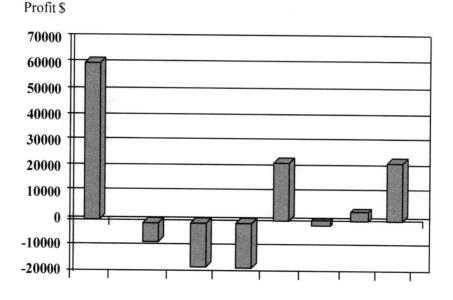

Sometimes the combination of all the clients served by one salesperson or one sales office yields an important picture of how "smart" that sales source is (or, conversely, of how smart the customers are). Different strategies for different situations can make significant contributions to the bottom line. This type of data presentation enables better sales and marketing strategies.

## Top 15 Customer's Profitability

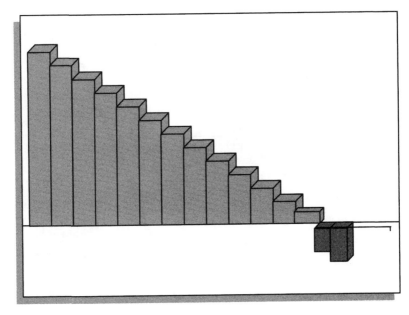

At some interval, customers should be reviewed on the basis of their profitability. Over time, those who consistently take away from the bottom line must be reconsidered. Why are you doing business with someone that you can't make a profit from? Some businesses have used this tracking method to flag those customers with whom it was time to renegotiate price increases and new contractual terms.

# Total Product Profits

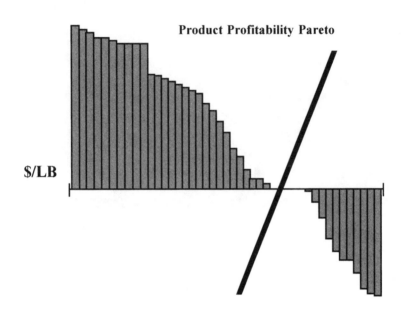

**Product Profitability Pareto**

**$/LB**

Product profitability can be viewed through many different perspectives. The same good business/bad business view is shown here in the relative performance for a company that had a number of different products produced in the same plant. Market conditions were always changing and one never knew (accumulatively) whether any product was making money until this type of executive summary was reviewed and explained. This information also provoked many cost improvement studies and more than one product elimination analysis.

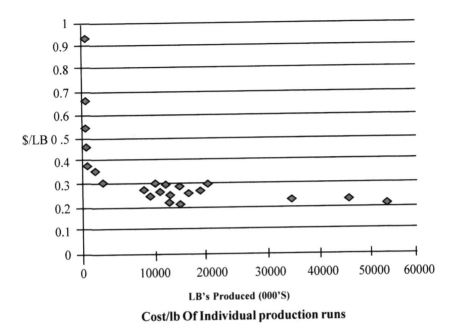

**LB's Produced (000'S)**

**Cost/lb Of Individual production runs**

Single products made in the same production facility demonstrate variable profitability. This annual history of one product plotted against the size of the production runs yields invaluable knowledge about setting a minimum production run size. That single piece of information has more than paid for all of the ABC work with one client.

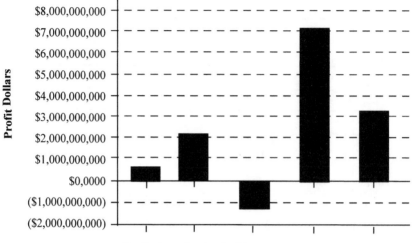

Compiling profit groups into end uses or other strategic market or organizational focuses often reveals relative contribution information not previously known. Clients have often
reorganized or restructured product support based on this
knowledge.

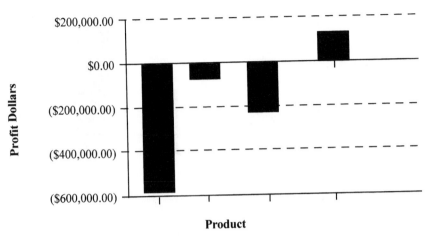

These figures represent typical portrayals of profit by product under various circumstances. These measurements are often used to reflect the result of efficient operations or to measure the change from a cost improvement activity.

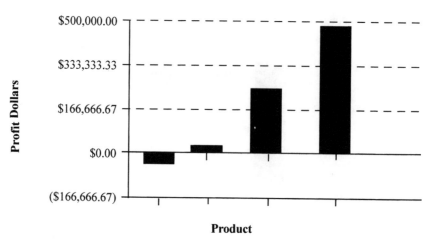

These figures represent typical portrayals of profit by product under various circumstances. These measurements are often used to reflect the result of efficient operations or to measure the change from a cost improvement activity.

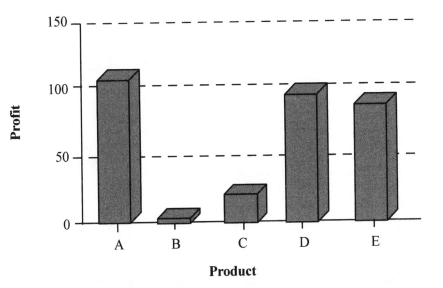

These figures represent typical portrayals of profit by product under various circumstances. These measurements are often used to reflect the result of efficient operations or to measure the change from a cost improvement activity.

| | |
|---|---|
| **Sales Unit Price:** | 0.9000 |
| **LBs to Sell:** | 100,000 |

| | | | |
|---|---|---|---|
| **Product Name:** | 2105 ⬇ | | .8554 |
| **Monomer Cost:** | .0000 | **Monomer Adj.:** | .0000 |
| **EU Name:** | Compounders ⬇ | | .0030 |
| **SM Type:** | Bulk Truck Indirect ⬇ | | .0700 |

| | |
|---|---|
| **State:** | TX ⬇ |
| **City:** | FORT WORTH ⬇ |
| **SP Code:** | 13P ⬇ |

**Standby Cost:** .0249

| | Unit | Gross |
|---|---|---|
| **Total Cost:** | .9284 | 92,840 |
| **Total Profit:** | -.0533 | -5,330 |

Calc

Exit

Knowledge of profit by product, coupled with inventory management systems and transportation cost data can provide an extremely valuable tool for the sales representative who negotiates "deals" with clients. This decision support was designed to be on-line, providing the ability to see the profit of any product sold at any price and delivered with a choice of freight systems to any destination. The ability to have this information while the deal is being made enables you to hold the salesperson accountable for the profit contribution you expect, not just volume of business.

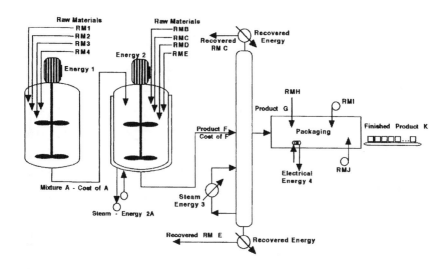

The marriage of ABC and distributed control systems allows a new type of process control variable: product cost. In this example, the ABC model of the process shown is run every minute and the results are trended just as other flows and pressures are measured. The results here were fed back to the control system and given to the operator so he or she could be held responsible for a targeted behavior. The use of calculated variables is accepted today, but the use of cost in process control is certainly innovative.

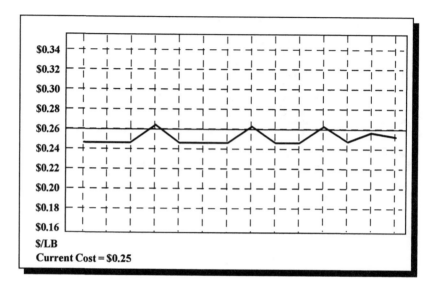

The marriage of ABC and distributed control systems allows a
new type of process control variable:   product cost. In this
example, the ABC model of the process shown is run every
minute and the results are trended just as other flows and
pressures are measured. The results here were fed back to the
control system and given to the operator so he or she could
be held responsible for a targeted behavior. The use of calculated variables is accepted today, but the use of cost in process
control is certainly innovative.

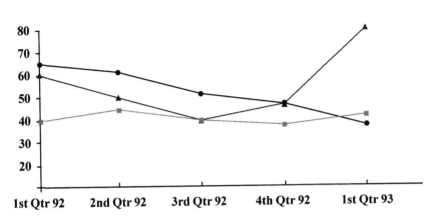

Knowledge = Based Decision Making

Tracking the impact of market and cost controls can be con-
fusing, but tracking behavior by product categories over time
can point out areas to investigate more closely or those that
deserve work in cost management.

## Improvement Targeting

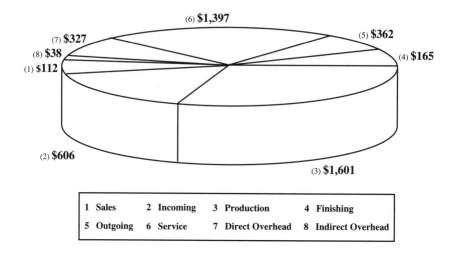

| | | | |
|---|---|---|---|
| 1  Sales | 2  Incoming | 3  Production | 4  Finishing |
| 5  Outgoing | 6  Service | 7  Direct Overhead | 8  Indirect Overhead |

The classic pie chart serves the purpose of pointing out those cost elements that are large relative to others. I am continually amazed at the number of investments that are focused on relatively insignificant cost elements, in the big picture. It is always beneficial to present summary data in such a way as to demonstrate the relative shares of the components.

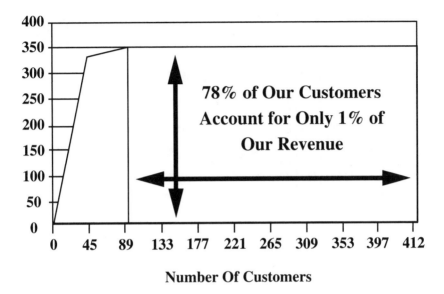

**Number Of Customers**

ABC measures the consumption of resources and costs it out for you. Order processing, and billing take the same relative amount of resources for a small order as for a large one. This summary analysis surprised us all and became a strategic measurement for efficient and effective use of resources in the support functions. Plan your business a little better, find less expensive ways to handle the bad business, and realize better profits.

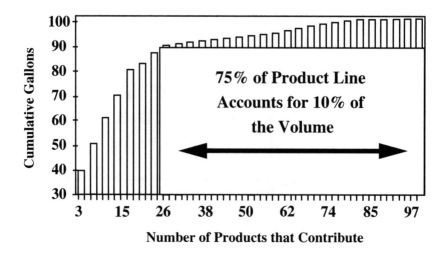

Product line management costs money. Keeping stocks of raw materials, infrastructure, and technology in place for seldom ordered products can be expensive. Using activity-based measurements for product life cycle and business performance contribution analysis is an excellent way to keep from giving away potential profits.

## Making Change Permanent
### "More than paying attention"

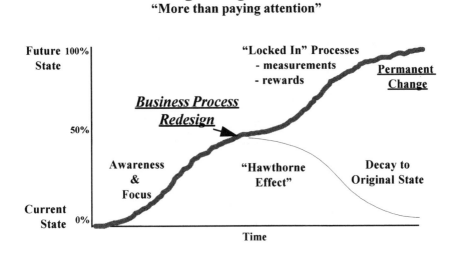

This figure depicts the overall performance curve, over time, of the improvements related to making a change in a measured process. The decay forecast was the way previous projects behaved, once the spotlight was removed from the improvement efforts, allowing human behavior to slip right back to the previous pattern. Measurements and incentives capture continued improvement in this plot of actual performance.

**Order Management Process**

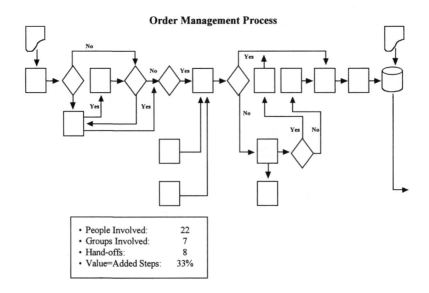

|  |  |
|---|---|
| • People Involved: | 22 |
| • Groups Involved: | 7 |
| • Hand-offs: | 8 |
| • Value=Added Steps: | 33% |

Activity-based costing requires documentation of the various steps in the process being measured. Evolution generally has created an intricate web of interconnected tasks with many handoffs between people who make some contribution (and also create major bottlenecks) toward the process flow that represents this function. We need to ask the following questions:

- How much resource?
- How much cycle time?
- Does every step contribute value?
- Can this process be streamlined, shortened, made more efficient?
- Can we accomplish the same thing faster, better, cheaper?

Using a flow diagram enables the ABC team to model the costs consumed and identify the factors that drive costs. It is also an excellent opportunity to reengineer the process.

## Order Center Cycle Time

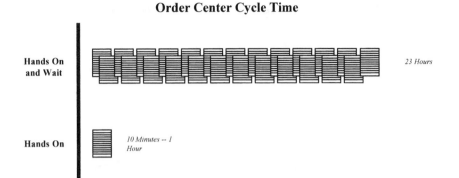

The classic measurement of process efficiency also applies to business processes. A review of activities in the costing effort often reveals the magnitude of the NVA (non–value-added) efforts on cycle time. These represent significant targets for process improvement. Magnitudes and strategic importance combine to help select those that should be reformed first.

# Raw Materials Consumption Trends

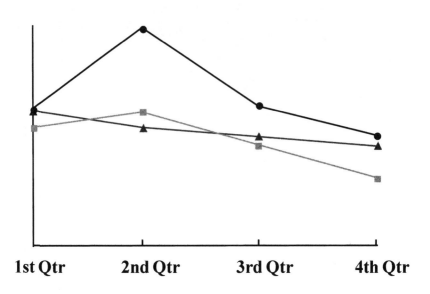

**1st Qtr        2nd Qtr        3rd Qtr        4th Qtr**

A measurement system related to cost must, by definition, capture the behavior of the raw materials consumed for each product. All too often I find good information on total raw materials consumed, but nothing detailed enough to tell me if one product consumes more than was expected (or perhaps is so difficult to make that much waste is generated). Track raw materials and look for trends. Plot them in total and by product; you may make some significant discoveries.

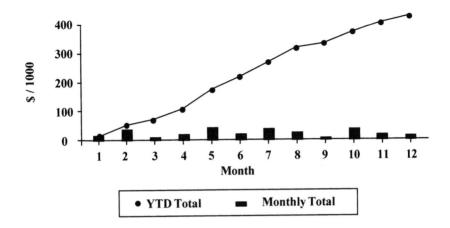

Another way of looking at single-product raw material consumption is the combined monthly and year-to-date graph. I prefer to set target levels on this type of chart.

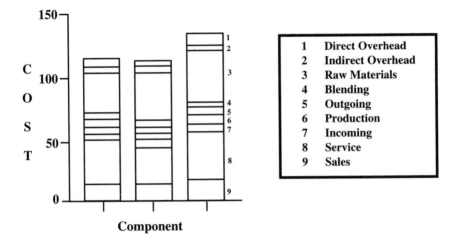

Charts that combine functions provide excellent diagnostic capabilities. This example used a client server platform to access a large historical database and supported a "point and click" ability to look for three levels of detail for a specific element of cost. The next screen shows the access to more detailed information on the blending costs of one product.

# Blending Cost

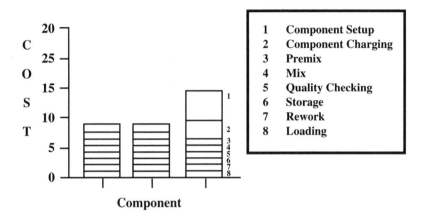

Component

The blending costs were made up of a number of tasks. Some were significantly larger than others and the same point and click capability allowed this user to drill down even further to explore why rework was such a large piece of the blending cost.

**Rework -- Time History**

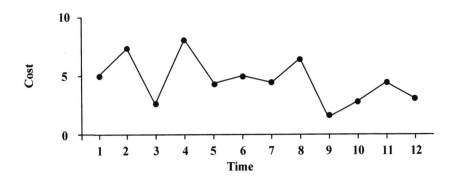

This time-history, which made up the net value represented in the previous figure, demonstrates some 400% variation. In the mind of a process control engineer, this variable is *out of control*. This behavior should provoke analysis if the magnitude warrants it.

# Inventory

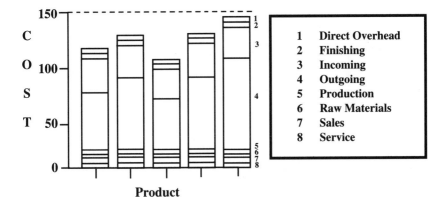

**Product**

Note the categories of cost that can be represented by segmented bar graphs. Too many cloud the facts, but this basic type of data presentation supports good diagnostic and decision support requirements. Better yet, this type of graphic can be achieved with current spreadsheet packages on the desktop PC, without costly custom software.

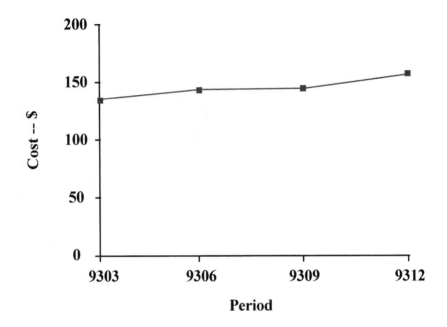

Trends are particularly easy to generate with the same PC tools. Trends are an important way to look at costs, as snapshots often represent a random move or behavior that does not represent a long-term trend or behavior.

| ▬ | | ₦ | ABC - REPORTS |
|---|---|---|---|

**File** **Import** **Reports** **Window**

**Process Cost Dock**

**Product Fully Burdened Cost**

**Product Profitability**

**Product Variable Cost**

**Product Total Cost**

**Price Module**

**End Use Summary**

I have never found a business in which everyone could agree on the same definitions or on the same formats for data presentation. Many software products (for example, this one from "Powerbuilder") allow you to use windows-like pull-down menus and to add to the number of applications you need to use, at will. This menu screen demonstrates a number of different ways one client looks at the same basic data.

# Glossary

## A

**Activity-Based Costing (ABC):** A method of looking at the collective costs of each business process within an enterprise

**Activity-Based Management (ABM):** The use of ABC information in the ongoing strategic and tactical events of managing a business

**Annualized Cost Data:** The average costs over a year's spending and production

**Authorization for Expenditure (AFE):** A request for approval to spend capital

## B

**Bar Charts:** Plots using vertical or horizontal bars to show magnitude

**Bell Curve:** The "normal" distribution of behavior showing that most samples behave on the average

**Business Plan:** A written definition of the expected performance of the enterprise, along with the strategy and plans for achieving both sales and production

**Business Planning Parameters:** Definition of the controllable and uncontrollable variables

**Business Process:** The elemental unit of a functional delivery unit within a business

**Business Process Reengineering:** The act of mapping each element of the process under study and redesigning (by consolidation and elimination) those that are non–value-adding and nonessential

# C

**Computer Integrated Manufacturing:** The use of systems technology to capture information from every aspect of the manufacturing business

**Control Variable:** The element of the process that is changed to make some target attribute change in the desired direction

**Cost Dynamics:** The change that occurs naturally in the behavior being observed

**Cost of Goods Sold (COGS):** A common term for manufacturing costs

**Customer Probability:** The contribution to the bottom line from the orders delivered to one specific customer

# D

**Data Reconciliation:** The act of checking results against another reference

**Dynamic Cost Moves:** The behavior of cost, on a frequent time basis, showing the variance of costs over time

# E

**Empowerment:** The assignment of information and authority to make decisions

# F

**Feedback:** The use of measurements downstream of a control point, for use in knowing whether a control action was of the right magnitude and in the right direction

**Forecasting:** Using extrapolation to project behavior into previously untested regions

# I

**Intrinsic Information:** Information that was indirectly included in the basic data and held value for the user

**Intuition:** The "gut" feeling regarding the evaluation of data that helps the cognitive thinking process

# L

**Life Cycle:** The normal period of time from introduction of the new product to the last sale and close out of production

# M

**Measured Cost:** Those costs attributable to the consumption of resources and measured by specific cost drivers (e.g., flows)

**Minimum Order Size:** Dimension that will provide enough profit to offset the startup expense

**Models:** Algebraic algorithms that represent the individual components of each business process, allowing calculation of an analytical value of their performance

# O

**Optimum:** Mathematical maximum

# P

**Paradigm:** Predictable behavior with which we usually respond; a habit

**Pareto Diagram:** A graph depicting ascending or descending order

**Process Control:** The automatic management of a single variable in a manufacturing process

**Product Mix:** The list of products and the amounts being produced during a fixed period

**Profit:** What is left over after costs are subtracted from revenue

# R

**Real Time:** The availability of information while something can still be done about it; may be seconds or hours or days

**Relational Database:** A repository of information that may be accessed by a number of different attributes

**Resultant:** The net value achieved after some calculation

**Revenue:** The income realized from a product or service delivery

**Rolling Average:** The average result of scrolling a fixed number of values, moved across an endless supply of data

# S

**Sensor-Based Measurements:** Value obtained from a device that counts or otherwise sends a performance measurement to an external readout system

**Strategic:** An action or plan that sets long-term direction toward a specific objective

**Sunk Costs:** Costs that are not recoverable despite any action taken

**Supervisory Control:** The management of multiple variables to achieve a specific complex objective

# T

**Tactical:** The actions or plans implemented to achieve short-term or immediate results

**Time-History:** A set of data or information that represents enough prior time slices to virtually reconstruct the historical performance of a variable or resultant

**Time Period (ABM):** The selection of a segment of time

**Time-Slice:** The instant of time in which a snapshot of data is collected

**Time Stamping:** The inclusion of the actual sample time for a piece of data

# V

**Value Chain:** The sequence of events that are involved in the upgrading of value

**Value System:** Those standards by which actions are held in esteem, relative to value

**Variable Costs:** Those costs over which control is possible (A CEO once said that he had the power to make all costs variable)

**Variances:** Deviations from the norm that occur with actual behavior

# Y

**Yield:** The percentage of product that is actually realized compared to the theoretical maximum

# Index